Having worked as a travel writer for the past decade, Nina Karnikowski now writes about travel that conserves, educates and uplifts more than it destroys, and aims to demonstrate through her writing how travel can help solve societal and environmental problems. Nina is the author of *Go Lightly: How to Travel Without Hurting the Planet, Make a Living Living: Be Successful Doing What You Love* and *The Writer Within: 50 Journaling Prompts to Inspire and Transform*. Her writing appears regularly in *Traveller* in the *Sydney Morning Herald, Condé Nast Traveller, Life & Leisure* in the *Australian Financial Review* and more, and she sits on the Conscious Travel Foundation's panel of experts. Recognising the power of creativity to generate sustainable solutions, Nina also mentors writers and creatives and teaches writing and creativity workshops. She lives on Bundjalung Country in the Northern Rivers region of New South Wales with her husband and dog. Find out more about Nina's work at ninakarnikowski.com or @nina_karnikowski on Instagram.

THE *Mindful* TRAVELLER

NINA KARNIKOWSKI

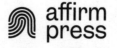

affirm press

First published by Affirm Press in 2023
Boon Wurrung Country
28 Thistlethwaite Street,
South Melbourne, VIC 3205
affirmpress.com.au

10 9 8 7 6 5 4 3 2 1

 A catalogue record for this
book is available from the
National Library of Australia

ISBN: 9781922930217 (paperback)

Cover design by Luke Causby/Blue Cork © Affirm Press
Cover image by Peter Windrim, shot at Salty Cabins
Author photo by Kat Parker
Typeset in Garamond Premier Pro by J&M Typesetting
Proudly printed in Australia by McPherson's Printing Group

MIX
Paper from
responsible sources
FSC® C001695

For Pete, who reminds me to look at the bugs, the birds and the butterflies when my head is stuck in the clouds. And for the bugs, the birds and the butterflies, which make this a world worth fighting for.

Instructions for living a life:

Pay attention.

Be astonished.

Tell about it.

Mary Oliver

Contents

PART ONE: STAYING   1

1   ICE *Awakening in the Arctic*   3

2   FIRE *Pausing on Minjerribah*   21

3   STARS *Hiking in the Warrumbungles*   37

4   MUSHROOM *Meeting the fantastic fungi*   49

5   ROOTS *Gardening the way home*   63

6   CORAL *Road tripping to the Great Barrier Reef*   81

7   RAINFOREST *Facing fear in the Daintree*   95

PART TWO: AWAKENING   **105**

8   ROCK *Feeling soliphilia in the bush*   107

9   SILENCE *Meditating towards myself*   121

10 WATER *Rising together in the floods*   137

11 TREE *Forest bathing in the Southern Highlands*   149

12 MOTHER *Connecting in the Kimberley*   163

13 COUNTRY *Listening to Tasmania's first stewards*   177

PART THREE: GOING   **189**

14 LEOPARD *Rewilding in Rajasthan*   191

15 WOMAN *Weaving a bright future in India*   205

16 MOUNTAIN *Seeking wisdom in the Nepalese Himalayas*   225

17 RAINBOW *Taking action on Heron Island*   241

A SHORT NOTE ON THE WAY FORWARD   249

ACKNOWLEDGEMENTS   253

Part One

Staying

1

Ice

Awakening in the Arctic

This is the trip that will explode my life, though I don't know it yet. The only thing I know right now is that I'm about to descend on the polar bear capital of the world. A tiny town called Churchill, on the edge of the Canadian Arctic.

From above, in the little rickety aeroplane, I can see spruce trees that have been buffeted so hard by the freezing arctic winds that one whole side of them has blown clean off. These stunted trees – named Krummholz trees after the German word *krumm,* meaning crooked or twisted – are my first taste of the strangeness and harshness of this place. I've come in the summer, knowing that at this time of year I'll see both polar bears and beluga whales – hundreds of the first, tens of thousands of the second. My stomach flips over itself with excitement as we start to descend. This is what I live for: exploring remote, far-flung corners of the world, where I can breathe the wild air and be bowled over by wonder.

Surely, there could be nowhere more full of wonder than Churchill, which sits right in the middle of the largest polar bear migration on earth. Eight hundred humans live here, but each summer about nine hundred polar bears congregate around town as they wait for Hudson Bay to freeze over. I can imagine nothing more terrifying, or more exhilarating. As soon as I heard about it, I knew I had to go.

Churchill is not a place for the faint of heart. Which, in truth, is part of the attraction for me. For the past few years, I've been wanting to toss myself into travel experiences that feel too big for me, pushing me to my limits and helping me break through internal barriers. I've been chasing trips that make me *feel* something – that remind me that I exist. I've hiked across passes of over 5000 metres to see Peru's Rainbow Mountain, travelled through eastern Mongolia in ex-Russian military vehicles to sleep in *ger* tents with nomads, bounced across the length and breadth of India searching for the truth of life, and ventured to the opposite tip of the world – to Antarctica – in an icebreaker ship. I've done all this to gather material to write compelling travel tales, yes, but also to slap myself awake, and feel brave and alive in a way I've never really felt at home. To pause the normal flow of things, as only travel can do, and take a kind of hiatus from my life.

When a travel assignment came up to this remote outpost, where winter temperatures drop to minus 40 degrees, and where the snow can get so high that people have to dig tunnels to reach their neighbours' houses, I couldn't resist. It seemed radical, and promised all the danger and expansiveness I couldn't find in my regular life, which, as I moved into my mid-thirties, felt increasingly like a corridor of shrinking and vanishing doorways.

Once our tiny plane has bumped onto the landing strip, my six travel companions – an all-female group of American and Canadian travel writers and agents, all of whom are strangers to me – and I are driven in a tiny bus into the tiny town. Churchill is set on a finger of land pointing out into Hudson Bay. The town is essentially just one long main road flanked by some low-rise stores and inns, with about ten residential streets branching out from the north side. On the way in we pass fields dotted with willow trees and tall grasses, purple fireweed and yellow avens, with the waters of Hudson Bay glinting beyond. Our driver tells us that while the bears are off the ice in summer, they often wander over these fields and into town. Locals here are full of stories about finding polar bears on their porches, in the back streets late at night and even in their kitchens, fossicking around for a snack.

In the overcast afternoon light, we pass buildings swathed in polar bear murals. They're part of an art project designed to spread awareness about the melting of the polar ice caps and the detrimental effects this is having on bears. There are polar bears swimming in arctic waters, polar bears cosied up with arctic foxes, polar bears wrapped in the neon green and purple northern lights. We pass a pebbly beach with a yellow polar bear signpost on it, a warning for visitors like us to keep our eyes peeled. We also pass the local recycling plant, which our driver tells us now has steel backing. Polar bears broke through the concrete wall in search of food last year, he says like it's nothing. It had to be reinforced.

~

It goes without saying that the eight hundred people who live in Churchill are a tough bunch. One of the toughest, though, is the owner of my home for the week, a log cabin called Lazy Bear Lodge that looks like an oversized scout hall. The lodge was built completely by hand by a polar bear tour guide named Wally Daudrich, a tall man with strong-looking hands, thinning grey hair and a gentle smile. It took him over ten years, using reclaimed timber from two forest fires. He's raised five kids here.

The lodge, with its huge open fireplace and wood-panelled walls hung with antlers (and a rather disconcerting polar bear pelt), is warm and cosy, but we don't stay long. Adventure awaits. After we've eaten a dinner of arctic char from the waters of Hudson Bay, our guide arrives: a young Canadian named Deb who moved here with her photographer husband two years ago, after visiting and falling in love with the place. Deb drives us to a nearby dock lined with candy-coloured wooden storage sheds. During the arctic summer, when the ice breaks up, around 60,000 beluga whales migrate here to Hudson Bay to feed, mate and give birth in the warmer shallow waters, and we're about to go out to meet them. My heart is thumping as I pull an insulated dry suit over my three layers of clothing and wriggle a full-face snorkel over my head.

We putter out onto the bay on an inflatable Zodiac motorboat. A floating blue mat, kind of like an oversized gym mat, is attached to the back. Once the boat has come to a stop, we lie on the mat belly down, and submerge our faces in the ice-cold water, some of which seeps in around the sides of my mask.

At first, I see nothing but the indigo waters of the bay. A few minutes pass, and then suddenly dozens of belugas, each about four metres in length, are swimming towards us. 'Beluga' comes from the Russian word meaning 'white', and the whales are indeed snowy white all over, their skin helping them camouflage against the sea ice. Their alabaster bodies glide towards us like majestic, gentle ghosts. When I squeal – partially in terror, partially in delight – one of them swims up close, peering at me with two black raisin eyes on the sides of its squishy white face, its mouth curved in a smile.

I jerk my head out of the water and pull off my snorkel, squinting in the arctic evening sunshine. The rational part of my brain recognises these creatures as playful and gentle. But I can't help being intimidated by their sheer volume and proximity. Right now, I'm acutely aware of how far from the rest of the world I am. There are no paved roads leading into Churchill. If anything were to happen to me, trains or planes would be my only way out.

'You're fine!' yells Deb, clearly sensing my panic. 'They're just curious. Try singing to them; it'll make them come closer!' Yes, singing. Belugas are nicknamed 'canaries of the sea' and are known for their loud, clear vocalisations, which they love to hear back from humans. I take a deep breath, remind myself that there's nowhere else on earth I can have this experience, plunge my head back under the water and start singing a song from *The Little Mermaid*.

It's embarrassing, sure. But with the mask on, no one but the belugas can hear me and, as I sing, they swim closer, turning their necks side to side as no other whale species are able to do, and peering inquisitively into my eyes. I breathe deeply and keep singing. Belugas have flexible, bulbous foreheads that can change shape, and they famously often look as though they're smiling. I smile back from inside my mask, and it feels like my entire body – my toes, my knees, my liver, my heart, maybe even my teeth – is smiling too.

I'd expected to see a whale or two, but they're gathering around us by the dozen, as curious about us as we are about them. Deb tells us there are hundreds of them around this area, and that this is the largest whale population in the world. When I sing, they sing back with a haunting series of clicks and whistles, chirps and squeals. These sounds help them communicate with other whales, and, in winter, help them find holes in the ice sheets so they can make it up to the surface for air.

They're completely entrancing, and I barely pull my head out of the water for over an hour. When I do, the sky has turned from tangerine to dusky pink, and the setting sun is throwing glitter across the water. The world feels brand new.

~

The next morning, we head out to look for polar bears. This time, we're on a boat called the *Samuel Hearne*, named after the first European to travel overland across northern Canada to the Arctic Ocean in the 18th century. Wally Daudrich from the lodge is leading the tour and I'm here with a few handfuls of other travellers. It's a bluebird day, and the sea is flat and still.

We're cruising along when, all of a sudden, Wally points calmly to the water and says, 'There, polar bears.' Just like that, as though he were pointing out a pigeon. Two polar bears are paddling alongside us like a pair of gigantic white puppies. We rush to the edge of the boat to watch their dinner-plate-sized paws pull their chunky, 400-kilo bodies through the water and listen to their loud snorts of exertion. Their snouts are raised in the air; their small, rounded ears sit just above the water line.

One of them looks over its shoulder at us and, just for a moment, I meet its eye, black and narrowed. The connection makes my breath catch in my throat. It's like a zoom lens has been placed over my eyes, and all I can see is that ebony eyeball fringed by wet white fur.

In that glance, I feel as though the bear is saying something to me. Is it 'I see you, friend'? Is it 'Back off, you're too close'? Or is it 'Please, can you help me'? I'm not sure. Up until this moment, polar bears have existed for me only in kids' story books, those 90s Coca-Cola polar bear ads and David Attenborough documentaries. Seeing these creatures that I've always associated with ice doggy-paddling and duck-diving through sun-spangled water is discordantly delightful – like seeing a monk on a mobile phone. We watch the bears climb onto the banks, covered in summer's tall purple fireweed, then lope along the rocky shore, sniffing the air with their mouths open to see where we are and what we're doing.

I can't stop fat tears – tears of awe, of joy, of wonder – sliding down my face.

~

Back in town, at the small visitor's centre, a guide is showing us around some exhibits about the area's ecology, and we start to learn alarming facts about what we just saw. He says the warming of our planet and therefore longer summers mean the ice on this bay, the primary habitat of the polar bears, now forms later and melts earlier. This means the bears' seal-hunting season is shorter, since there are lots of escape routes for the seals in the melting ice, and they have less time to feed and put on weight. Some bears may not get the fat they need during winter to survive through summer, and surviving females without enough fat won't produce cubs, both of which equate to declining populations. The bears are hungry, which I guess is why they're doing things like breaking through concrete walls of recycling plants and getting into people's kitchens to find food. I walk slowly around the exhibits, my hands becoming clammier and my heart thumping faster with each brutal fact I learn. A single black eye flashes across my mind like a lightning bolt.

The most devastating part is that the bears have no way of protecting themselves from the effects of climate breakdown, says our guide. They have done nothing to cause it – unlike us humans, driving gas-guzzling cars, flying around the globe, constructing buildings, making too many clothes and too much plastic and doing thousands of other harmful things – and they can't protest or change their behaviours or do anything else to stop it. Only our actions will have an effect.

When we walk back outside into the late afternoon, my footsteps are heavy with sorrow and shame. The world seems somehow, instantly, less beautiful.

~

For the community living here, the polar bears are not a faraway issue. Bears are literally in their backyard, and can be encountered at any time. Wally tells me about the day he found polar bears playing on his kids' swing set. A local Inuit guide shows me a video of one sunning itself on his back porch. Locals leave their houses unlocked so anyone can find shelter quick smart if they meet a stray bear. We visit the 'polar bear jail', a holding facility on the outskirts of town where wayward bears are held for a while if they cause trouble or threaten anyone's safety, before they're relocated. I'm assured there have only been a handful of bear attacks in town over the past fifty years. Still, walking back to our lodge from the pub one night, staying in the middle of the road and not cutting corners to avoid bumping into a lurking bear, is an experience I'll happily never replicate.

What I am happy to repeat, as many times as possible, is visiting the belugas. Early on our final morning we head out across Hudson Bay on another Zodiac. Deb trails a small underwater microphone behind us. We listen to the beluga's high-pitched, supernatural-sounding whistles, clicks and moans and watch their white bodies glowing neon green beneath the water, mimicking the northern lights that often flicker across the sky here.

Every so often we glimpse an expressive face – a curious black and white eyeball, a swipe of mouth that always seems turned up in a cheeky smile, a white brow furrowed in curiosity.

Before we head back to shore, Deb decides to drive the boat past a particular spit of land, just in case there's a polar bear there. The waters are choppy and about five bucketloads of icy arctic water end up in my lap on the way there. But I soon forget all about that, because when we get to the point, we see a big female polar bear snoozing on the rocks, with a baby snuggled up behind her. It is impossibly cute – cuter even than those memes you see on Instagram of smiling baby hedgehogs being bathed in people's kitchen sinks. We sit there for a long time, watching the cub occasionally peer out from behind its mum to sniff the air and see what we're up to, before it eventually falls fast asleep. All I can think is, *I want to still be able to see these majestic creatures in ten years' time.*

~

At the airport, I google to find out more about the plight of the polar bears. I discover that polar bear litters in the Hudson Bay area are indeed getting smaller, and that every polar bear population in the world has seen a change in their access to sea ice in the last thirty years. For each day earlier in the season the arctic ice breaks up, research says, one day is lost for polar bear mothers to rebuild their stores of energy for summer. Scientists have also found that for every week the ice breaks up earlier, the bears come ashore 10 kilos lighter.

I google the belugas, too, and discover that despite the numbers we saw, conservation scientists consider them to be near-threatened, also mostly because of rising global temperatures. If ocean temperatures continue to rise, the belugas' migratory routes and the availability of their prey will be hugely affected. When the ice melts, the nutrients held inside it, which contribute to the entire marine food chain, disappear. Because belugas are near the top of that chain, if they are out of balance, it's a powerful indicator that there's something going on with all of life in the ocean. The message underpinning all of this is that the arctic holds the key to the future of our entire planet, and when things change here, everything is at stake.

I lower my phone and sit there in the cold, busy terminal, watching hundreds of people rushing off to hundreds of planes. We are all contributing to the melting of the ice, whether we're aware of it or not. Now that I am aware, though, having seen what's happening in this achingly beautiful place that most people on the planet will never see up close, I have a responsibility to do something about it.

~

When I get back to my home in the northern rivers region of New South Wales, everything feels off kilter. Like the world has been tipped a few degrees and I can't quite find my balance. Like there are lengthening shadows everywhere, blocking the light.

It's not as if the polar bears were the first instance of environmental degradation I've ever seen on my travels. Two years ago I travelled to Borneo, where I drove through hours upon hours of palm oil forests that had replaced the old growth forest homes of the orangutans, and visited an island where, every morning, the beach was completely covered in plastic trash swept in from the ocean. Last year in Antarctica, I learned that 90 per cent of the world's seabirds now have plastic in their systems, and that there's now virtually nowhere on earth that microplastics, which filter into our oceans and our food chains, are not. I felt heartsick after witnessing these things, but often at a loss when it came to doing something about them. The problems just felt too immense, and it was easier to turn away and keep living my best life. After the Arctic, though, it feels as though these experiences have clogged up somewhere in my soul, like hair in a drainpipe. The grief is pooling up and overflowing into my body and brain, and I no longer feel able to continue on with business as usual.

I do all the things that usually help me recentre – scribbling in my journal, going to yoga classes, running on the beach, taking long baths – but I can't get back into my usual groove. My thoughts keep circling back to the melting ice, to our warming planet, to how much we humans have messed everything up and how uncertain and deeply troubled our future seems. Friends ask, 'How was the Arctic?' And I smile and tell them about singing belugas and swimming polar bears and the enchanting mystery that sits at the top of the world. I don't want to be depressing.

Inside, though, it's like a light has been flicked off. Smiles are difficult, I can feel my shoulders drooping and my footsteps falling heavily when I walk, and when I look in the mirror my eyes are dull. I self-flagellate with documentaries and books and articles about the climate crisis, reiterating things I vaguely knew before, but which have a different resonance now. One night, my husband Pete and I watch Al Gore's 2006 documentary *An Inconvenient Truth*, which drives home the message that it's our obsession with burning fossil fuels that's causing climate change. Since 1970, Gore says, the extent and thickness of the arctic ice cap has basically dropped off a cliff. In 2006, we had already lost about 40 per cent of the ice cap. Al Gore warned then that within the next fifty years it would be completely gone during summertime, and we are now halfway through that fifty-year time bracket. And as the latest research from NASA shows, arctic sea ice is now shrinking at a rate of more than 12 per cent per decade, compared to its average extent during the period from 1981 to 2010.

This, of course, means terrible things for polar bears. One scene in *An Inconvenient Truth* shows a skinny, computer-generated polar bear desperately paddling through arctic waters trying to find some ice to rest on, while Gore's voiceover describes how polar bears are now drowning after swimming distances of up to 60 miles to find ice. Watching the scene, my hands become sweaty again, and I get a sinking feeling in my stomach. A single question prowls around the dark corners of my brain: what on earth have we done?

Later, in maybe a year's time, I will find myself in a doctor's office seeking a referral to a psychologist. I will describe my lack of focus, my looping thoughts about imminent planetary collapse, and the sense of impending doom I feel when I read news sites full of reports about wildfires, floods and species extinctions. He will tell me more and more patients are coming to him with this sort of eco-anxiety. I will discover nearly six in ten young people are experiencing this, according to a large study in the UK in 2021, exacerbated by our sense of powerlessness at being able to effectively act on such a huge global issue. The diagnosis will make me feel immediately less alone, and less crazy.

For now, though, I muddle through. I drive to the shops, I put on the washing machine, I switch on the lights, I turn on the heater, I cook dinner. I think, when I do these things, of burning coal and oil and gas, and how I am betraying the one planet we've got. I think about polar bears and belugas. I read a statistic about international flights ballooning from 70 million in 1960 to about 1.4 billion today, a figure expected to reach three billion by 2050, and think what an awful lot that is for our fragile planet to handle. I think about the hundreds of flights I've taken in the past eight years working as a travel writer – about thirty-five a year on average – and of the part I am playing in this ecological unravelling.

I discover online carbon calculators, plug in my international air travel from the past year, and learn that my carbon footprint, just from that air travel and discounting all the other activities I do, is over 40 tonnes. The average Australian household, I learn, has an annual footprint of about 15 to 20 tonnes a year, and to limit global warming to 1.5 degrees by 2050, the UN says we need to limit our per-person emissions to 2 tonnes a year. I'm burning twenty times that – twenty times! – just from flying, and I feel sick about it. The calculator tells me that if I want to offset my emissions, I'll need to restore around 3000 square metres of natural habitat, which is roughly the size of twelve tennis courts.

When I tell a friend about this, she says to stop worrying. It's not my problem. She says the whole carbon footprint idea was created by British Petroleum in 2004 to make the public think climate protection was their responsibility, not the fossil fuel industry's. Which I later discover is true. I know there's a much wider, woven conversation to be had about all of this, and that ultimately it's up to our governments and powerful corporations to stop pulling fossil fuels out of the ground in the first place. But still, I can't unsee what I've seen. I can't unlearn what I've learned. And to refuse a sense of personal responsibility now just feels wrong. I think of the meme 'It's just one plastic straw ... said eight billion people.' The power of collective action is undeniably strong.

So here are the paradoxes I now hold. I believe travel to be a mind-expanding, heart-opening, vital thing that connects people and cultures and provides jobs and important income for 10 per cent of the world's population. But I also know that the travel industry is responsible for about 8 per cent of the world's carbon emissions, as well as degraded wilderness areas, overtouristed towns, the erosion of local cultures and more. I believe that by travelling the world we can fall in love with it and be inspired to act on its behalf, and also that if we don't act, we can become more a part of the problem than the solution. I believe that movement is essential to who so many of us are, but also that there won't be a world worth seeing in years to come if we don't start seeing it the right way now.

And that, I decide, is exactly what I need to do. To stand still for a while – six months, at least, without setting foot on a plane – so I can figure out how to move around the world in a healthier way. To really look at the work I do, to really look at myself, and ask if I'm doing the right thing by the planet I'm so passionate about exploring.

~

After I've been home for about a fortnight, I read a series of news stories about the teenage Swedish climate activist Greta Thunberg. She's sailing from Plymouth to a UN climate summit in New York on a solar-powered yacht to make a stand about the climate crisis and demand immediate emissions reductions. If a sixteen-year-old can take such powerful action, then I sure as hell can do something too.

A couple of weeks after that, Pete and I attend the worldwide Fridays for Future climate action school strike, demanding political action on the climate emergency and instigated by Greta Thunberg, in our town. We march through the streets alongside hundreds of kids and adults holding placards emblazoned with slogans like 'Raise your voice, not the sea level!', 'Don't be a fossil fool', and 'There is no planet B'. The looks on the kids' faces, the strength of their voices, says it all: they want the future we have had, one without the constant threat of environmental catastrophe. They want a liveable planet. The eyes of future generations are upon us. We must all do whatever we can.

~

One morning, I wake before dawn. A light rain is drumming on the roof. I slide the lounge room glass doors open and pad out onto the verandah, welcoming the cold, damp air. Sitting on the outdoor couch, I light a candle and look out at the grandmother fig tree towering over the dark garden. I want to be part of her life, not part of her destruction.

I stand and walk down our back steps, my bare feet pressing into the wet grass and the dark, damp earth below. With raindrops falling onto my skin like little kisses, I think about how our separation from the earth is what lies at the heart of this ecological collapse. And about how coming back into a deep, loving, entwined relationship with the living world is what will ultimately be the cure. More than that, though, I think about how I don't want this to be a thought. I want this to be an action.

2

Fire

Pausing on Minjerribah

The first action I take is to start saying no. This is difficult for me. It is for many women I know. We are taught to say yes, to oblige. We are taught to be polite rather than to be brave. We are taught to make other people happier than we make ourselves.

Now that I have decided to take some time out from travelling, though, and because the universe likes to test us, the assignments start coming in thick and fast. An invitation to Papua New Guinea arrives first, as fascinating and enriching a place as I have ever been, then another to western Mongolia, which has been on my wish list ever since visiting the east of the country five years ago. An invitation to Thailand, too. Then comes one that almost tips me over the edge.

I'm working in my home office, the late spring sun slanting through the window, spilling onto my desk and beckoning me out into the day. I'm tapping away at my keyboard when an email pings into my inbox.

'I feel like a shocking temptress,' begins the message from one of my editors, 'but an invitation to a nineteen-day private jet trip across Africa has just arrived. Do you think you could take the assignment?'

Three days with the gorillas in Rwanda. Two days exploring Ethiopia's ancient rock-cut churches. Three days visiting the South African wine lands. On it goes. It is, from all angles, the travel assignment dreams are made of. Except that, as I read the email over a second and third time, I notice my stomach isn't churning with excitement as it once would have. Thanks to my post-Arctic climate research binge, I now know that not only do private jets generate more greenhouse gas emissions per passenger than regular commercial flights because there are so few people onboard, but also that a high-speed luxury trip like this would have minimal positive impact on local communities. It's run by an international company, so most of the income would leak out of the countries we'd visit and into foreign pockets. And how much could anyone really learn about Ethiopia or Rwanda, nations with incredibly complex cultures and histories, from just two days on the ground? Not much. I take a deep breath, lean forward in my chair and write back to my editor, politely declining the assignment.

Pete can't believe I said no. I can't either, to be honest, and I can almost feel my 21-year-old self kicking me in the shins for it. But I'm glad I did, even though I'm worried – very worried, in fact – that I'm throwing a grenade at my career, which I've worked ferociously to build and maintain. How does an international travel writer work and make money if she isn't travelling? Besides, as Pete points out, if I'm not going on that assignment, another writer will. That carbon will still be burned, and that story will still be told, so what difference does it make if it's by me or someone else?

He's right, of course. But I'm starting to question more deeply what my role as a travel writer is, or should be, beyond just getting paid and telling good stories and having a great time. When I started out, the job felt like a gift from the universe. For a long time, all I wanted to do was chase that glamorous, jet-setting life, filled with interesting people and places and stories, as far as it would take me. My first assignment was a meditation retreat in Bali, and the following week I was in New Zealand flying to vineyards on helicopters and driving around in a Jaguar and eating at one of the world's best restaurants and staying in very posh hotels. I wondered how many children's lives I must have saved in a past life to get this level of positive karma. I loved exploring and writing stories, I loved thinking about how many people I was encouraging to live a life less ordinary, and I secretly loved splashing my lavish, adventure-filled life across social media.

As the years passed and I started seeing more of the world, though, a sense of responsibility crept up on me, slowly but surely, like the grey hairs that started creeping onto my head when I hit my early thirties. Maybe it was maturity, maybe it was the result of being exposed to more and more places that were so different from the one I called home, but I started wanting my stories to mean more and to shed light on some of the deeper issues facing the places I was seeing. And now? Now that I'm recognising how much of an impact all of us voracious travellers are having on the world we love exploring, I want to tell people about that, too.

In the afternoon, Pete and I take our dog, Milka, for a walk. She's a maremma: a 40-kilo, fluffy white wolf of a thing, who stops to sniff every bush, every lamppost, every peed-on patch of grass. Our rented house sits at the edge of a small hinterland town, skirted by farms and bushland. It's a sweet town where honour-system farm stands and community library boxes dot the streets. At this time of day, when the sun hangs low above the hills and casts a golden glow over the eucalypts that line the dirt road we are following, hundreds of flying foxes wheel across the sky on their way out to feed for the evening. We walk in silence, watching them overhead and keeping an eye on the top of the eucalypts, where most days we see a koala or two wrapped around the branches. Pete walks ahead. I watch him hike past the river and up the red-dirt path, and I think about the restlessness that has defined our life together so far.

We were married ten years ago, on a cold winter's eve in June, in a glass-walled restaurant on Sydney Harbour. I wore an embroidered dress my mum had bought me. I was twenty-seven, the first of my close friends to be married, but Pete and I were determined that saying 'I do' would be only the beginning of a grand adventure.

As a sort of statement of intent, we left for a six-week honeymoon to East Africa two days after the wedding. We danced all night on an island in Mozambique, we went on safari in Zimbabwe where we were almost trampled by a herd of wild buffalo, we took a helicopter ride over Victoria Falls as rainbows arched across the sky. Afterwards, we walked to the lip of the falls, bowing our torsos out into the abyss, breathless with exhilaration as we peered into the canyon below.

Two years later, just when we'd started going to house auctions and fielding an increasing number of queries about when we were going to have kids, we opened an escape hatch by moving to India for a year. I wrote travel stories for the Australian newspaper I was working at, and Pete got a job as a graphic designer on an international magazine. When we returned to Australia, Pete decided to quit his graphic design career to become a winemaker on his family's farm, and we moved to the country. Meanwhile, I continued travelling for about a third of the year to places as far flung as Antarctica and Namibia, Mongolia and Peru.

We were chasing risk and romance, running towards places and existences that felt exciting and fresh and full of hope and wonder. But we were also running away. Away from other people's and society's expectations. Away from the 'quick catch-ups' and get-togethers. Away from endless conversations about real estate and babies and the minutiae of daily life.

Rather than being hard on our marriage, Pete and I have often joked that being apart for chunks of each year was the secret of our marriage's success. Now that I've temporarily paused that part of my work, though, and the more humdrum realities of life are all we have, I begin to wonder how much of a joke it really is.

Spending a few weeks apart while I hike a mountain in sub-zero temperatures in Japan or learn about the plight of the polar bears in the Arctic isn't the hard thing. Arguing over which of us has done more vacuuming that month, or who walked the dog more this week is. I have always wanted a version of life that was historically denied to women – one filled with autonomy and adventure. I watched my mum struggle under the weight of balancing her work as a schoolteacher with the household chores, and with giving me and my older sister the best chances she and my dad possibly could, and I saw how the frustrations that accompanied that balancing act could be the thief of spontaneity and excitement. I think it's partly because of that that the debates in my own life about whose job it is to clean the bathroom, and about whether that task is of equal or greater value to mowing the lawn, have often made me feel as though the walls were slowly closing in on me.

As we reach the top of the hill and I watch the man I love patting the dog I love in the day's dying light, I wonder whether staying put will help us see these daily realities in a new and different way. Not as a trap, but as an invitation into a greater sense of stillness and rootedness, and a deeper intimacy with each other.

Maybe we don't need to crisscross the globe to find wonder. Maybe we don't need to burn masses of carbon to be awed. Maybe, with the right eyes, we can be as floored by beauty in our own backyards as we can anywhere in the world.

~

Australia is on fire. By the end of the first week of the year, more than seven million hectares of bushland have been burned, the equivalent of about seven million sports fields. Twenty-three people have been killed, and half a billion animals have perished in our state alone. Thousands of homes have gone up in flames, and all their possessions and memories with them.

It's the worst bushfire season on record. Every state in the country has had fires raging, but the biggest burn is along stretches of the southern and eastern coast, where we live. There has been talk of a hot, dry weather phenomenon called the Indian Ocean Dipole being the cause of it, but the overwhelming consensus is that rising levels of CO_2 are the root cause. Australia has been getting hotter over recent decades, and this year, new temperature records have been set, on top of a long period of drought. Scientists have been warning us for decades that this hotter, drier climate will mean more frequent and intense fires, and now we're living in the apocalyptic future we never really believed would come. We are all praying. For rain, for salvation.

I turn on the news one afternoon, which I've been trying not to do, and the images look like they're from the centre of hell. Red skies over Sydney, black billowing plumes of smoke covering coastlines, neon orange flames devouring bushland. Thousands of decimated homes, hundreds of people huddled on the beach while their towns burn behind them. The most heartbreaking images, though, are of the koalas. Koalas with burned fur and skin clinging desperately to firefighters; koalas with bandaged paws and red-raw eyes; koalas being handfed water by wildlife rescuers and volunteers. None of it seems real.

Vast swathes of bushland are burning around our home, so close that embers are falling into our backyard, burned leaves drifting like black snow from the sky. Pete gets a ladder and climbs up on the roof to clear the gutters, and we shut all the windows against the toxic smoke that the Australian Medical Association is warning us could be fatal. Text messages fly around our group of friends. Some have already evacuated; others are staying put and risking their lives to guard their homes. We are all aware of how fast things can escalate with wind and fire. We are all terrified. We are all aware that bushfire season is far from over.

We are also all furious with our government. This catastrophe is making it abundantly clear that they've been doing an abysmal job of protecting us against the effects of climate breakdown. Australia is one of the world's biggest per capita greenhouse gas emitters, and we have a clown of a prime minister who, three years ago as treasurer, walked into parliament with a big grin and a big black lump of coal and said, 'This is coal. Don't be afraid, don't be scared.' But we were not afraid. We were dumbfounded and confused and wondering how our country could be run by such a blind fool.

This question has become a war cry now. Our carbon-intensive economy is what has got us into this mess, a fact that becomes clearer with every hectare of bushland that burns, every koala that dies. Our government does not care, and is promising little in terms of emissions reductions, while still subsidising new 'clean' coal power stations that are anything but. We are falling short. Very short. And because of that, our country is now in flames.

~

A few days later, I'm booked on a train to go to Sydney. The journey takes about twelve hours more than a plane would, but knowing that trains use up to 50 per cent less fuel than planes, I booked a train seat in an effort to try to cut down my emissions. The train, however, is cancelled because of the catastrophic bushfires, and so I wind up taking a plane after all. The very thing I was avoiding. I sit in my window seat, drinking tea from a paper cup because I forgot my Keep Cup and feeling like an enormous failure.

I look out the window and over the tops of the clouds, a view that used to make me want to cry with happiness, but today makes me want to scream and shout. It makes me want to crawl under this seat and hide until the world doesn't feel like it's going to explode anymore. But I breathe, I breathe, I breathe. I remember that I, that we all, need to do the exact opposite. To look these tragedies square in the face, and to be attentive to what happens in a world where we have forgotten how to take care of the earth.

~

The wine bar Pete runs has been eating him alive. Too many late nights, too much stress, too much money going out and not enough money coming in. Between that and the stress of the fires, we decide we both need a break, and head to North Stradbroke Island, a ninety-minute drive and a short ferry ride away from home. I decide to switch my phone off and leave it at home for the four days we're away. I feel anxious as soon as the screen goes blank, but I know it's what's needed. I read recently that these days we take in as much information in a day as Shakespeare took in over a lifetime, which I guess is why my brain feels like a swirling, throbbing mess such a lot of the time.

The moment we drive onto Straddie, it's clear we've made the right decision. The island's local Quandamooka Aboriginal name is Minjerribah, meaning 'island in the sun', and it is exactly that. We drive twenty minutes along dusty, sun-basted roads lined with spiky pandanus palms and native balga grass plants, and I immediately feel my pulse start to drop.

Within minutes of arriving at our campground, tucked beneath eucalypts and paperbarks, we've pulled on our swimsuits and are walking the two minutes along the path through the forest that leads to the beach. We are greeted by an empty white arc of sand, lapped by turquoise waters, bookmarked by a rocky outcrop the colour of eggshell. It's a good windbreak, so we lay towels out beneath it, slather on sunscreen, pull out our books and let the afternoon ooze away. Dipping in and out of the warm water, walking across sand that sighs beneath our steps, lying in the sunshine as salt crystallises on our skin and stiffens our hair. Later, we picnic on the headland, watching a few surfers dance over the last lazy waves of the day as the sky turns amber, then purple, then indigo dark.

By 7.30pm, we've shucked our bodies off the headland and are climbing into bed. I'm no night owl, but this is absurdly early, even for me. There are moments of FOMO. Shouldn't we be stargazing? Reading? Wine-drinking? Until we remember that this is exactly what we came here for. To try to find some empty space in the chaotic symphony of

30

our lives. The Arctic made me crave a less dissociated relationship to the natural world, but I know I can't get that without first finding some space and quietude within myself.

The rest of our time on Minjerribah passes in soft slow-motion. There's more swimming and sunning. More reading and napping. A bit of hiking, a bit of sex. All the best, most essential things, and quite the opposite of all the things we tell ourselves are essential – the emails and meetings and phone calls – as we rush through our warp-speed lives.

On our final morning I walk alone to the empty beach, crossing the hot sand to a small teepee someone has built from paperbark boughs and scraps of hessian. I sit inside it, out of the blaze of the sun, looking out through the opening at the seam between the sea and the squeaky blue sky and thinking, *This is all I need*. To take things slower. To get salt on my skin, and sun in my hair. To sit down on the sand, push my hands into the earth and ask the simple question: what do you need?

~

By March, all the fires in our state have been extinguished. It's the first time there have been no fires here since July last year. While one disaster has finished, however, another has risen up in its place. The Covid-19 pandemic has been slowly gathering strength around the world, and now the first Australian has died. Lockdown is announced in our town. The day that happens is the day my first book – it's called *Make a Living Living* and profiles twenty-six creatives from around the world who have made a living doing what they love – launches into bookstores which all have their doors firmly shut. Pete has decided his bar won't make it through and has put it on the market, and any hope I had at the end of the fires is quickly slipping away.

I go to bed with my thoughts churning. I often wake up in tears, and the clawed hand of a migraine grips my skull most days. My worries have worries, and they are eroding my capacity to do things – especially work. I'm still writing the odd travel story from past trips, and am writing stories and giving interviews about creative living in line with my book, but I feel far less capable than usual. I walk around in an anxious fog, consumed with disquiet about our collective future. I am a ghost woman mourning for her dying planet, and for life as it was, now that everything has so irrevocably changed.

Trapped inside our house, all I want to do is flee. I sit at my desk and, instead of working, I read stories online about how many people around the world don't have homes to shelter in, which makes me guilty about feeling like a caged animal inside my own.

I sit on the back deck one morning, looking at the fig tree and scribbling down some thoughts to help ease my anxiety. Running away has been my way of coping with fear, ever since my late teens, when I started having panic attacks.

The first one happened when I was sitting on a crowded bus on my way to high school. Suddenly, the paper I was reading for my final exams started to blur, the letters rearranging themselves on the page. There was a roaring in my ears, like a wave rolling into shore, and I started having difficulty breathing. The bus was hurtling down the freeway when I begged the driver to stop. He reluctantly dropped me on the side of the freeway, and I sat on the kerb in my green chequered school dress as the morning traffic rushed by, looking at my trembling hands and wondering how I would explain to my friends that I had gone mad.

After that first panic attack, they kept coming. I think they were caused by the pressure I was putting on myself to get perfect grades in my exams, combined with a more general tendency I've had since I was very small towards worrying about the future and pleasing everyone except myself.

Without any real guidance on how I might deal with this terrifying thing that sometimes swept over me, that made me feel like I was slipping out of my body and into a vortex that took me up, up and away, they continued on for years. Then, at twenty-one, I moved to France for a year as part of my university degree, and discovered what a healing balm going far away could be. After that trip, any time life became confusing or too much, I would go away to seek answers.

Now, of course, I can't do that. I had already chosen to stay still, but now it's no longer a choice, and I cannot break away. I am being forced, we are all being forced, to bear witness to the pain, the loss and the grief that is part of this unfolding. I must change myself, not my place. I must find a way to be in the same place differently, not escape to a different place with the same self. I must learn to pay generous attention to the world I live in, right here at home. The message Earth is sending us all could not be clearer. Stay put. Go slow. Be present.

~

I'm in the garden, listening to a podcast from the poet Pádraig Ó Tuama. Lying on my back looking up at the searing blue sky, I listen to his lilting Irish voice talk about how we must reach for whatever tools can most help us do the almost shamanic work that's needed right now, to transform our grief into light. 'What might it be like to have a practice that helps us move away from things that distract us, and settle down into the simplicity of looking at mystery through the lens of a lamp?' he asks. 'What is the warm, butter light of a lamp that lets you hold yourself together? Whatever that might be, turn towards that.'

My lamp, I know, is writing. It is my own sacred ceremony. Every morning I write and I write, by candlelight and as the sun rises, fear retreating with each letter formed. My lamp is also lying next to Milka, my hand resting on her beating heart, my fingers weaving through her fur. It's listening to the sound of my own breath, wiggling my toes in the grass, staring at the trees for a while and saying to myself, 'Look at that,' while watching some funny bird.

I must do these things because I need to keep the fear at bay. As painful as this time is, I doubt there will be a return to 'normality' afterwards. In April I come across an article written by Arundhati Roy in the *Financial Times* that reads, '[The pandemic] offers us a chance to rethink the doomsday machine we have built for ourselves. Nothing could be worse than a return to normality.' She is right. This strange, liminal time can also be a time for reimagining and remoulding our lives. If we can let the sadness we're feeling not undo us, but fuel us, we can get clear on what we need to let go of and what we want to call in when we re-emerge, blinking, into the new world.

The pandemic could also, I'm realising, be a kind of portal into a more just and healthy world. I read that these lockdowns have decreased global carbon emissions by more than 8 per cent, to the lowest level in a decade. *The New York Times* reports that residents in northern India can see the Himalayas more clearly than they have for three decades due to the dramatic drops in air pollution since we've all stopped flying and driving and consuming. Studies in America are showing that in just a matter of weeks, the songs of sparrows have recovered the acoustic quality they had decades ago, and I've been seeing images of deer grazing on traffic islands in Japan, and marauding elephants wandering the streets in China.

The world, it seems, is rewilding itself. It could be our chance to rewild ourselves, too. Our chance to remember what we have forgotten: that there is a sacred, primal bond between the earth and our own bodies, and that if that bond is severed, the chaos that has been surrounding us these past few months will be the consequence. The living world will ultimately endure, but if we don't remember how to pay proper attention to it, and come back into a deeper, more engaged and balanced relationship with it, we may not be so lucky. It's we who will become extinct if we don't pull the cotton wool out of our ears and learn to listen to the language of the earth again.

3

Stars

Hiking in the Warrumbungles

The sky is high and blue and the sun is hard and bright as Pete and I set out along dirt tracks lined with white gum trees and spinifex grasses. Occasional bursts of wildflowers – purple pea bushes, golden wattles, white paper daisies – dot our path. It's late winter and the air is fresh, but the hike is steep and soon we're peeling off our woollen jumpers as we stop to catch our breath at a lookout point. There, we get our first glimpse of the Breadknife – a 90-metre tall, 2-metre thin slice of rock gracefully piercing the sky, the remnants of volcanic eruptions more than thirteen million years ago.

We arrived in Warrumbungle National Park, home to one of our state's most impressive hikes and Australia's best stargazing, a few hours ago. Coming here was a last-minute decision, a kind of ripcord I'd needed to pull when our house, our suburb and our town had all started growing over me, shutting me in. Last week we had dinner with some close couple friends we adore, and after hours of talking about real estate, other people and their children, I ended up at home in tears, filled with frustration, and also guilt, for finding that kind of conversation with people I love so empty and dull.

A couple of days later I was raging to Pete about the stagnancy I was experiencing, which felt like a fungus growing slowly through my body, my cells and my blood. I'd been trying to stay grateful for being able to walk outside in clean air, for having a home to shelter in, for being healthy. But after almost a year of no movement, I missed the world and my old life with a sometimes terrifying intensity.

'Well, babe, why don't we just ... go somewhere?' Pete said that day, stopping to grab my hand and pull me close to him on our morning walk. He looked into my eyes with his sparkly blue ones and tried to break this downward spiral I was talking myself into. Lockdowns were over for the time being, and we could indeed go somewhere inside our state. I'd been telling myself my travelling life was over, that the dreams I had built for myself were gone. But the truth is, I was still – am still, will always be – a traveller. Just because I cannot leave the country, something I want to do far less of anyway, doesn't mean I have to let all the colour run out of my life.

Yesterday we hired an old red campervan, packed it full of sleeping bags, pillows, pre-made meals and warm clothes, and started the nine-hour drive west. The van was the cheapest one we could find – so cheap, in fact, that just before we left the house the horn started blasting for no apparent reason and Pete had to yank the cord out from underneath to disable it. No matter. As soon as we were out on the open road, I could feel my chest opening, feel the sky above me opening, feel the whole world opening like a giant bay window. It felt like Exit Mould had been sprayed over my entire body, the fungus retreating with every kilometre of tarmac we put behind us.

~

Below the Breadknife is a far less intoxicating sight: tens of thousands of charred trees, remnants of the monster wildfire that ravaged Warrumbungle National Park in 2013. Ninety per cent of the park's vegetation was decimated, and with it most of the koala and wallaby populations. These blackened trees are a potent reminder of how Australia is suffering, both from the impacts of climate-induced wildfires and from the lack of Aboriginal burning.

During the bushfires, I read a lot about this on news sites and in *National Geographic*, which Mum buys Pete and me a subscription to every Christmas. I learned that, for over sixty thousand years, Australia's First Nations people have known that if the land is burned gently, the wildfires that will inevitably come later won't be as destructive. But since Australia was colonised and the land was stolen from Aboriginal people, their land care practices have largely gone with them. Only now, it seems, are we recognising how deeply destructive this has been, for all of life in Australia.

As we continue walking up through the bush, our boots crunching along the dirt paths and the magpies warbling softly in the eucalypts, I wonder how, if we don't prioritise Indigenous land management, and if we don't all find ways to come back into right relationship with the earth, we'll stop these catastrophic weather events from getting worse. We already lost three billion animals in the Black Saturday bushfires. How much more are we willing to lose before we make the changes we need to make?

These questions roll around inside my head as we walk, and I let them. I have always loved walking for exactly this reason. It lets my thoughts spool out until there's nothing left of them but their echo. Then, and only then, can the landscape rush in and take over. Filling my whole body and my whole mind, leaving me feeling completely *inside* the world in a way I rarely do otherwise.

This is the point I reach, after about three hours of hiking, when we climb a thigh-burningly steep set of rough sandstone steps up to the peak. My mind is clear and still, and there's nothing to do but stand in reverence before the endless expanse of the valley. Pete and I sit down on the warm rock, the wind whipping around us. In the local Gamilaroi Aboriginal language, Warrumbungle means 'crooked mountain', and we sit and watch the clouds play over the otherworldly rock formations rising up from the ancient landscape like giant's teeth.

This was all once under water, and when I squint, I can see the effect that water has had on the landscape, rolling out like waves in front of me. I close my eyes and imagine what life might have been like when this landscape was formed, thirteen million years before humans even existed. I listen to the wind, to the sound of my own heart beating, to the heartbeat of the land beneath me. I remember that there is no separation between the land and my own body, between the soul of the land and the soul of myself. It is the simplest act of reconnection there is, standing on the earth and loving it, but it is profound.

~

By the time we get back down to camp, the sulphur-crested cockatoos are screeching in the treetops. Night is coming. We need to make fire quickly before the cold sets in. I'm grubby and sweaty from the day's hike so I run off to take a quick shower in the communal bathrooms. They're basic, but the water is hot and hard. Afterwards, I pull on thermals, jeans, a jumper, a puffer jacket and ugg boots. Walking back to the fire, I'm already warm as toast. Pete has always made great fires. I stop about 20 metres back from our camp spot to watch him at work. My heart swells as I watch this person I love feed twigs to the flames and adjust logs. He will always keep me warm.

We cook up some gnocchi on the camp stove, then sit out by the fire, gazing up at the wide spill of stars. The Warrumbungles is Australia's only 'dark sky park', which means there's zero light pollution and the night sky is thick with bright stars. We lean back in our camp chairs, sipping ginger tea and pointing out the constellations and shooting stars, then Pete slips off to bed and I stay there. Full of stars. Full of earth praise. Wondering how I could have forgotten how good this could be.

My mind drifts back to Jordan's Wadi Rum desert, another landscape of craggy outcrops and vast, wild spaces, where Pete and I travelled three years ago. It was 35 degrees under the beating midday sun, and we'd been hiking all morning, but our Bedouin guide, Ali, was insisting we drink hot tea. Crouched over an open fire beneath soaring walls of sandstone, he boiled tea with sprigs of rosemary and thyme and innumerable tablespoons of sugar. We protested: it was too hot; it had been since dawn when we'd woken in our Bedouin camp. But Ali was born and raised in this desert and would have none of it. He dismissively waved a hand and promised the scorching liquid would, in fact, cool us down. 'Tea, fire, silence, nature, these are the best things,' he said then, pressing the cups into our hands.

At the time, sipping that tea and experiencing the truth of his words, I vowed never to forget them. But in the flurry of the next couple of years, of hurtling around the globe at light speed, of searching for stories and wonder and myself, I had forgotten. Tonight, though, I remember.

Tea, fire, silence, nature. They really are the best things.

~

I have never really felt as though I belong in Australia. I was born here, Mum was born here, and Dad came here when he was two, but Mum's parents were born in Hungary, Dad's in Russia and Poland. I never felt like I – the girl with the weird surname, with the weird food in her lunchbox, with the parents who spoke weird languages at home – quite fitted in.

When, at sixteen, I went overseas for the first time, to France on a school trip where I stayed with a host family for a month, I finally felt like I was home. Everything was alien, but at the same time familiar. And ever since then, I've felt that home, for me, has been wherever I am in the world – that it's a place inside of me, not outside of me.

Now that I'm grounded in Australia, though, I'm asking myself more and more: what does it mean to be from here? And why have I always felt so haunted by this place I call home, but don't really feel *is* home?

Identity is a complicated thing, particularly in colonised countries. And this land that I was born on, this land that my grandparents fled to when war was ravaging their countries, is land that was stolen in brutal and violent ways. On this land, Indigenous people were raped and murdered, enslaved and incarcerated. On this land, some of the worst crimes against humanity happened. On this land, entire communities were wiped out by gunfire and disease, herded off cliffs, burned alive. I was not taught about these atrocities at home or in school. And, I'm ashamed to admit, I didn't do much to learn about them myself until recently.

How can I feel at home here when it's not my land? How can I heal my relationship with this landscape, when it comes with such tense associations? I don't know the answer to these questions. But just asking them, and just being out here on the land, might be a start.

~

It's first light when we wake up in the van, and the windows are foggy from our warm breath meeting the cold air. Last night we discovered that this van is about 30 centimetres too short for Pete, so there was a fair amount of tessellation that had to happen before we went to sleep. As I wriggle out of my sleeping bag and pull my ugg boots on to go to the bathroom, I discover that the front of one of them melted when I was resting it against the side of the fire last night.

None of this matters, though, once we're out under the sharp winter sky, gulping lungfuls of crisp, cool air and making tea on the camp stove. Less than 50 metres away, dozens of eastern grey kangaroos are fossicking in the grass and scratching their bellies, the morning sun catching in their whiskers and grey-brown fur. This place is reviving us, and we both feel effervescent, awake and *alive*. Ready for anything and in love with the world.

We pull on our hiking boots and backpacks and go for a morning bushwalk. When I stop to put my hands on a singed trunk and feel the charred bark beneath my fingers, I don't feel sad about the bushfires. Not today. I look around at the thickets of wildflowers and the lush greenery sprouting up everywhere, and I feel kind of hopeful. Nature has the power to fight back, and to rejuvenate itself. It has the power to rejuvenate us, too.

Later, back at camp, we decide we want to be closer to the earth. We grab an old blue and white poncho that Pete's mum, who passed away four years ago, gave him and toss it over the dry grass under a gum tree, then flop down on it to read with nothing but the rustling leaves and the occasional magpie song as our soundtrack. We promptly fall asleep for two hours, something I don't think has happened since about 2010.

When I wake, I blearily look down at the last page of the book I was reading before I fell asleep. It's Nikki Gemmell's *Why You Are Australian*. I found it in our suburb's street library a couple of weeks ago when I was feeling heartsick for the world, and felt it was kismet. 'In this age of accumulation, simplicity is the key,' reads the page. 'Shed skins. Find spareness. Travel light. It's exhilarating. Being lighter, stiller.'

It makes me think of a tarot card I pulled the other day. I've used tarot cards for years whenever I'm in search of some guidance. After shuffling and splitting the deck, I drew the Tower card – an image of a big white cedar tree being hit by yellow lightning and surrounded by angry red flames against a dark sky.

'The well-rooted tree that's been growing strong for decades is crashing down around you,' read the description of the card. 'Your world may feel like it's literally falling apart, and you didn't see it coming. Even though this phase is painful and confusing, it will be over soon. You'll look back and feel grateful things changed course. You might even see it as a personal breakthrough in the end.'

The world is indeed collapsing around us. And while I do feel that we needed to wake up and be pushed into a revolution, it is still deeply painful. There is so much waving goodbye at the moment, every day a different element of our old life walking out the door. My career as I knew it. Pete's bar soon to be sold. And, just last week, Pete's family's farm sold off, where we lived together for four years of our life.

At the same time, there is a sense of renewal that accompanies all this loss – lotuses arising from the mud.

When I travelled to Namibia for work last year, I had a wonderful guide and driver named Nestor, with whom I spent almost every waking moment of the two-week trip. We hiked through the wilderness and up the world's tallest sand dunes and met the indigenous Himba tribe and explored remote desert towns together. He told me stories about his life and his children and his beloved country that will stay in my imagination forever. We kept in touch after the trip, so I know he is struggling far more than I am during this time. Because of the lack of tourists visiting Namibia since Covid, his salary has been cut by 75 per cent. He has three children to support, one of whom he's putting through university; he has rent and car payments to meet, and no government support to help him do that. He's about to lose his car, and I'm not sure how he will get back on his feet without it.

And so, last week, I set up an online fundraising campaign and wrote a post on social media asking for help for Nestor. 'This is a time for all of us to act in reciprocity,' I wrote, 'and to give back to the people who give us so much when we travel … May we learn to look after the collective as well as we look after ourselves.'

I thought maybe I'd raise $100. But almost $1200 was donated by dozens of people – friends, but mostly strangers – who wanted to help Nestor. As it turns out, people can be heartbreakingly gracious and benevolent. Especially in times of crisis.

When we lose some things we love, I think, as I look up into the canopy of shimmering gum leaves, we find other things to love. Like the kindness of strangers, that we may never have otherwise known was there. Or like this moment, right now. Lazing on a rug with a book in my hands, Pete snoozing beside me, the land I was born on throbbing with the same energy as my own body.

4

Mushroom

Meeting the fantastic fungi

When things fall apart, we often do strange things to wrest back control of our lives. Me, I've started paring everything back, peeling away the layers of comfort so I can see more clearly and be less distracted. I've signed up to do a 'buy nothing new' year to challenge my consumption habits and to save money; I've stopped eating meat to try to reduce my carbon footprint; I've limited my news consumption to ten minutes a day so I can stay informed without getting overwhelmed; and I've even stopped drinking alcohol for a while. I'll probably reintroduce these things at some point, but for now I'm pulling away these crutches so I can confront my more murky feelings head on, rather than running away from them or numbing out like I usually would. I want to get myself clear, so I can figure out what the world needs from me.

I call a beloved old high school friend, who has been living in LA since we were eighteen and who I turn to whenever I'm seeking unorthodox advice. Flopped on the couch in our lounge room, I tell her I'm trying to get closer to the world around me, that I want to rekindle that sense of wonder and love I felt for the world as a kid. I tell her these lines from Lao-Tzu's *Tao Te Ching* keep ringing in my head: 'Love the world as your self, and you'll be able to care for it properly.'

She doesn't tell me I'm crazy.

She tells me I need to take magic mushrooms.

Now this isn't a revolutionary idea for me. I have tried psilocybin, the psychedelic compound found in certain magic mushrooms, quite a few times. In our circle of friends and in the region we live in, it's common to come across it at parties. On the occasions I've tried it, I've had a small amount, and it has always made everything a bit more sparkly, a bit hyperreal. Fairy lights and fireworks become brighter; the details of people's faces and plants get sharper. I've never had a big dose before, though, and it kind of terrifies me. I worry about whether my brain will be strong enough to handle it. My dad's brother is schizophrenic, which made me fearful about how drugs could tip hypersensitive me over the edge. But this time I'm not thinking of this as a drug, I'm thinking of it as medicine. Medicine I hope will help me see the place I live in in a new way, so I can feel less of a need to constantly seek out new places.

Psilocybin therapy is becoming more widely accepted, and there's renewed interest in psychedelics as potential treatments for various mental health issues. This has become especially true since the American author and journalist Michael Pollan came out with his bestselling book *How to Change Your Mind: the new science of psychedelics* a couple of years back.

Pollan's book explores what Mexico's Mazatec indigenous people, who have a long and rich history of using these mushrooms as a sacred medicine that they referred to as *Teonanácati* or 'flesh of the gods', have known for centuries. That these little brown naturally occurring mushrooms can change human consciousness and heal people of all kinds of things, from depression and anxiety to anorexia and OCD, to addiction and even the fear of death. Psilocybin does this, says Pollan, by breaking down our brain's 'default mode network' – the part of our brain that houses our 'self' and the stories we tell about ourselves. By letting go of that and loosening our grip of the whole idea of self, the mushrooms help us see things differently. They help us to move past old beliefs and biases and patterns, so we can zoom out and see the bigger picture – see the whole of the earth, even – and put things in perspective.

The most interesting information I've read by psychedelic researchers, though, is that psychedelics and the mystical experiences that accompany them are now being proven to influence pro-environmental behaviours (or PEBs as the studies refer to them) that involve protecting or conserving the environment – things like buying second-hand items or switching to a vegetarian diet. Since psychedelic experiences increase the connectedness and empathy we feel with nature, the PEBs they elicit become more internalised and powerful, leading to longer lasting sustainable action.

I've also been reading in the journal *Nature Medicine* about how neurochemistry is the language through which nature communicates with us, and that nature is trying to tell us something important by way of psilocybin. I want to hear what that is.

As it turns out, so does Pete. When I put the idea to him – that we take a *proper* magic mushroom trip, with a clear intention and making sure the setting, intention and dosage are just right – he's not only up for it, but says one of his barmen can source the mushrooms for us. So while Pete's busy organising the dosage, I deal with the setting. Knowing that the mushrooms will work best if we're surrounded by nature and far away from people, I book us in for a weekend at an off-grid cabin surrounded by bushland about thirty minutes' drive from our house.

~

Two days later, we're driving down a winding road to the cabin, the spring breeze rippling through the open windows and filling the car with birdsong. We turn and bump along a dirt track snaking up the side of a hill, until we reach the black timber cabin. It cantilevers out of the hill like a giant eye looking out over the 40 acres of bushland beyond, which we have pretty much all to ourselves. Inside the timber-clad lounge room, there's a potbelly fireplace and tall glass doors that slide open to the long, wide deck, which has a bathtub set into it. It is perfect.

We're here for two nights, and we've set aside the first one to just relax and sink into the space. Pete reads while I soak in the tub, then I read on the shaded daybed while he cooks a pasta dinner. Afterwards, we lie in each other's arms, stargazing on the deck and listening to the tinkle of the frogs in the waterhole in the paddock below. A bushwalk late the next morning, a lazy lunch, then we're ready.

The mushrooms have come in a squat finger of chocolate, divided into four pieces that are one gram each. We split the bar in two, and hold half each in our hands. This is not something we're doing for fun; this is a medicine and it's important that we set an intention for the trip. We sit on one of the steps leading down to the deck, set a timer for ten minutes, and meditate on what we want from the medicine we're holding in our hands.

Teach me what you need to teach me, I ask.

Trust. Let go. Be open, I hear.

When the timer goes off, we both eat the bitter, earthy chocolate, then flip through a coffee-table book about eco cabins while we wait for the mushrooms to kick in. After about twenty minutes, I'm reading a page about a tiny house in Japan when it suddenly seems like the most absurd, hilarious thing I've ever seen. 'Why ... does it *look* ... like that?' I ask Pete through hysterical hiccups of laughter. When he tells me it's just a normal cabin, like all the others we've been looking at, that itself seems hilarious, and I double over with laughter. At the same time, I start to feel nauseous, a sudden roiling in my stomach. I lie back on the round day bed, which feels like a safe, protected cocoon, and look at another page of the book to take my mind off my stomach. There's a picture of a cabin surrounded by bushes, but the bushes are moving in the breeze. Wow. It's a little scary, so I snap the book shut and drop my head back and look up at the sky instead. My body doesn't seem to be as *present* as it was five minutes ago. It feels difficult but not impossible to move, and my mind just wants to be up in the sky and the trees.

In the sky, I see diamond-shaped fractal patterns, and I suddenly understand that the sky is built. Created. Not just a blue nothingness, but a collection of atoms that have come together to create something beautiful – and it does look especially beautiful now. The sound of the insects and birds is loud, like the volume has been turned up a few notches. When a distant car or motorbike drives past, something I wouldn't have noticed normally, it sounds cacophonous and wrong – man-made, mechanical, and out of step with everything. So much sonic diversity gets drowned out by human activity.

There's a black metal fence at the end of the balcony, about a metre high, but when I focus on it, it rears up and grows higher. It seems horrible – why on earth would anybody build a fence anywhere, I wonder, closing all that natural beauty out? The fence seems to be getting higher and closer, towering above me and bearing down on me. When I tell Pete I wish it would stop coming so *close*, he holds out his hand and tells me to come to the edge of the deck to look at the bush. I'm only about two metres away, but it feels like kilometres. Eventually, I manage to stand, and when I reach him and follow his pointed finger out through the trees, I see a field in the distance that looks almost cartoon-like. 'It looks like an Ewok village,' I say, and we both agree that it is a magical glen and wonder how we didn't see it before. Pete watches intently and sees a hive of activity happening over in that glen. There are caravans and little people and a pagan ceremony happening, he says.

We drift back to the round day bed, and when we look up at the trees again, they seem to be dancing and waving at us. Not waving, actually, but clapping. Every time a bird sings, the trees shake their leaves in response.

It seems to be a kind of applause. We are mesmerised by this concert, and we are certain of the communication that is happening between the birds and the trees. *The birds need the trees*, I think. *And the trees need the birds. We all need each other.* The interconnectedness of the whole planetary system comes rushing towards me in that moment, and I keep thinking, *My god, this is always all around me – why don't I pay more attention to it? The world is just waiting for me to see it.*

Whenever I close my eyes, images appear on the insides of my lids, as if they were a screen. Pete puts on some music, not our wedding song but a song by the same artist, and I see me and Pete as cartoon skeletons dressed in wedding clothes, walking down the aisle. When I start to panic about these images and my lack of control, I remind myself to just stay surrendered and curious, and open to whatever the mushrooms want to show me. I discover that just changing my physical point of view by closing and opening my eyes, or looking in a different direction, changes the experience completely. Like switching the channel on the TV.

After some time – a couple of hours, I suppose – the intensity of the experience lifts a little, and everything softens and becomes more dreamy, like Vaseline has been swiped over my lens on the world. The sunset is the most beautiful, spangled sunset we have ever seen, and it looks like apricot glitter is drifting down from the sky. When I look up into the clouds, I see a vagina. Specifically, I see *my* vagina, and me being birthed out of it. I am the baby that emerges, sweet and fetal, and then that baby becomes a mother, and that mother is also me – in a rocking chair, holding two small babies. I feel so peaceful watching my future self like this, contentedly rocking the babies in the chair, with her face tilted towards the horizon.

Everything is poignant, everything is flooded with meaning and emotions. I go to the bathroom, walking over a rug with a geometric print that dances beneath my feet. I turn on the shower – I'm not sure why – and the water that comes out is thick and solid. I can see each individual water droplet and they are like diamonds. *Water is as precious as diamonds*, I think, and quickly turn the tap off. I don't want to waste a droplet.

Speaking of I, there is still a 'me' in this experience. We haven't taken a high enough dose to obliterate the ego, to completely break down the wall between ourselves and the world around us. But I feel I can see over that wall properly, for perhaps the first time in my life, and understand the animating spirit that exists in all living things. I understand that we are all – trees and birds and insects and clouds and me – a mass of vibrating molecules, all connected through some kind of cosmic consciousness.

When I get back from the bathroom and look out at the gold-dusted grass below the cabin, I see with great clarity that I need to be with it. And that I need to be naked. I take off all my clothes, pull the pink doona off the bed, wrap it around myself and start to walk barefoot down to the lawn. 'Will you be okay?' asks Pete as I walk out the door. The grass seems very far away, even though in reality it is right next to the deck. But my underlying feeling is I will be okay. *Everything* will be okay. Nature will take care of us.

I walk down the pebble pathway, toss the doona to the side and stretch out flat on the grass, cool and soft beneath my skin, letting the earth hold me. I look up and see flying foxes heading out to feed for the night. They are huge, and I can see the shape of their wings. I lie there thinking about everything that has happened this afternoon, about what it all means. Then a thought comes to me that is not my own. Not a thought exactly, but a voice in my head that says, *Just let it be beautiful.*

'I just need to let it be beautiful!' I yell up to Pete, who's still sitting on the deck, which doesn't seem quite so far away now. Overanalysing everything will not help me, and I am not in control of anything anyway, so I may as well *just let it be beautiful.* Which I suppose is another way of saying I just need to love the world fiercely, and let that love lead the way.

Pete nods, like the thought has already occurred to him. I feel a pinch on my skin and look down and see there are ants crawling all over my naked skin. I don't brush them off, though. They need me and I need them, and we are actually one and the same. I feel intensely grateful for the ants, for the flying foxes, for the trees, for the sky, for Pete, for my parents. For everything, actually. Gratitude is the thread that connects us all: I feel certain that the ants, the flying foxes, the trees, the sky, Pete, my parents are all grateful for me, too. I feel a sense of belonging to the web of life, unlike any I have felt before.

Many more things happen over the course of the evening, some of which can't be easily explained in words. We listen to music, including our favourite Ravi Shankar song, and I experience the music as if it is being played inside my body. As though it is my body, as though I *am* the music. I look at a candle flame at one point, and that also is my body, and I also am the flame.

All of this could sound like the ravings of a lunatic who is very high on magic mushrooms, or could sound like the truth as spoken by someone who has had their blinkers taken off. Blinkers that were put on when I was very small, which tell me I'm separate from and above nature. Now that they have been pulled off, I finally understand. I *am* nature. My aliveness is the aliveness of all things. If nature suffers, if koalas burn, if trees burn, if disease ravages communities, if hurricanes and earthquakes hit on the other side of the globe, we all suffer, because there is no separation. These mushrooms have been a portal back into a kind of primal knowing.

As far as transcendental experiences go, as someone who has spent a good fifteen years meditating and practising yoga and seeing various healers and travelling the world to find answers to my spiritual quandaries, this has beat them all.

It has been a powerful mystical experience, one that has shown me the life beating through all things, and that has allowed me to feel a universal love and wholeness that just doesn't feel accessible in everyday life. Even though by the next morning, everything looks just as it did before – the magical glen that we were so enchanted by yesterday, for example, turns out to just be a gully with a road running through it and some excavation – everything is also forever changed.

'I feel as though my brain has been rewired,' I tell Pete as we pack up to leave, and he agrees. Later, when I'm back home and he's at work at the bar, he texts me that he feels like the guy from *Limitless*, the 2011 sci-fi film where Bradley Cooper discovers a pill that gives him boundless mental power. Clear, relaxed, untethered. Completely reset. I get it.

I remember that a friend's copy of Michael Pollan's *How to Change Your Mind* is still sitting, half-read, on our bookshelf. I pull it out and turn to the dog-eared page where he describes his experience on psilocybin.

'All it took was another perceptual slant on the same old reality, a lens or mode of consciousness that invented nothing but merely (*merely!*) italicized the prose of ordinary experience, disclosing the wonder that is always there in a garden or wood, hidden in plain sight – another form of consciousness "parted from [us]", as William James put it, "by the filmiest of screens."'

Goosebumps ripple across my forearm. *Italicized the prose of ordinary experience.* That's exactly what this medicine has done. It has lifted the veil, and now that I have seen what's behind it, and feel as though I have had messages directly communicated to me from the more-than-human world, I have more motivation to fight for it.

'Maybe to be in a garden and feel awe, or wonder, in the presence of an astonishing mystery, is nothing more than a recovery of a misplaced perspective, perhaps the child's-eye view,' writes Pollan, 'maybe we regain it by means of a neurochemical change that disables the filters (of convention, of ego) that prevent us in ordinary hours from seeing what is, like those lovely leaves, staring us in the face.'

Now that I'm back in the real world, struggling through those 'ordinary hours', as we all are, I want to find a way to stay in this present, alive state. To keep this child's-eye view, and stay aware of all the magic that surrounds us, all of the time. I don't want to miss so much of life. I don't want to spend life in a trance, stuck behind a screen, worrying about the state of the world rather than just getting out there and doing something about it. And maybe if I *was* doing something about it, I would feel less frustrated by those everyday conversations with our beautiful friends. Because any irritation I feel at other people's apathy is actually irritation at my own apathy.

'As our eyes grow accustomed to sight, they armour themselves against wonder,' Leonard Cohen wrote in his 2011 book *The Favourite Game*. Now, though, I feel that armour has been pulled away, or at least part of it has, and my eyes are wide open. At a time of ecological collapse, these little brown mushrooms are important messengers.

What I notice, in the days and weeks afterwards, is that I have less fear and anxiety. It isn't completely gone, but I do have this underlying feeling of *okayness* that I didn't have before. Like the universe is taking care of things, and I don't need to white-knuckle life quite so much. I feel more dropped into my body than I did, and I've retrieved some level of freshness and spontaneity and creativity that feels like who I really am. What I guess I'm trying to say, as cheesy as it sounds, is that I'm living life more from a place of love than of fear.

Mostly, though, I notice that I'm more present to the world around me. That sense of connection with all things, and between all things, remains. On a Sunday, two weeks later, I'm going for a morning run when I notice a flock of white egrets wheeling across the sky, their wings perfectly etched against the blue, and I stop to watch their elegant ballet. Then my eye drifts over to the top of a stand of camphor laurel trees and I notice how the sunlight is caught and twinkling in the scooped leaves, like little pools of water. The communication that I saw between the birds and the trees is less dramatic than what I experienced at the cabin, but since I've seen it once my brain now understands that it's happening all the time, between all things. And if there's one understanding I want to hold on to from our mushroom journey, it is this.

5

Roots

Gardening the way home

I'm on my knees in our back garden, hands clammy inside thick gardening gloves, knees damp with soil, bare shoulders warm with afternoon sun. I'm holding a weeding knife called a hori hori, something I had no idea existed until a month ago and now can't imagine living without, and pushing its steel blade into the dark soil. Four baby lettuces sit beside me, and I'm about to plant them in the two-by-one-metre garden bed beside our deck. Which has, as of today, become my food-growing training ground.

Like millions of others during these pandemic times, I've turned to the garden for solace. When we bought this house a few months ago, in a quiet cul-de-sac between the river and the sea, the garden was a disaster: a thick tangle of lantana taking over the front garden, fallen and overgrown trees in the backyard, with termites building small towns in them, a whole lot of rubbish – kids' toys, mugs, crystals, fishing nets – embedded in the soil for reasons neither of us could fathom. First, it was all about damage control. Hacking out the lantana, turning over the soil, endless weeding. Now, though, we're finally ready to embed ourselves into this piece of land. We're ready to start planting.

~

My first memory of gardening is of my dad. I am sitting in my baby-blue childhood bedroom, looking out the window and watching Dad tend our small but abundant garden. He cuts back a fuchsia bougainvillea bush with some red-handled gardening shears, then stands back, hands on hips, surveying his work. He never wears a shirt when he gardens, and his skin glistens with hard-work sweat. I watch him appraising the plants, the lemon tree in the far corner, the staghorn suckering onto the jacaranda, the jasmine tumbling down the fence. I wonder what he sees there that I do not.

Whenever Dad was in the garden, he seemed lost in his own world. Quiet and observant and completely at peace. My mum and sister and I would giggle about his level of focus. But the older I get, the more I want what I know he found in there. This period of stillness is giving me a chance to find it.

I pick up a lettuce and push it into the hole I've made in the earth, patting the damp soil around the base to secure it. At a time of great uncertainty, it feels soothing to do something so simple, which I know is doing no harm. Something that will nourish both me and the earth.

As I plant the rest of the lettuces, my mind drifts to a young American woman I interviewed for *Make a Living Living* a few years back. When she was eighteen, her mother was murdered by her father. It was a trauma so intense I couldn't imagine anyone overcoming it. But she turned to the land, and eventually it helped heal her. 'Each time I planted something, I felt I was bringing my trauma to the soil, and it was turning it into food. That was so healing,' she said.

I'm certain this is what we're all doing now, during this gardening renaissance. Bringing our pain to the soil, pushing it into the earth and letting it alchemise into flowers and food, nourishment for our bodies and souls. We're taking something intangible and painful, and turning it into something tangible and healthy.

We are all gardening our way back to ourselves.

~

The more time I spend with my hands in the soil, the more I want to learn about gardening. Even though Pete farmed for years professionally, I want to have some autonomy, so I've signed up to a volunteer farming program in our town. I'm hoping both to learn more about growing food and to meet other aspiring green thumbs. This morning is my first session. The program is held on an 80-acre farm and as I walk across its paddocks from the car in the bright morning light, I'm as nervous as a kid on the first day of school.

Two young female farmers, both with long ropey hair stuffed under akubras and almost vibrating with good health, welcome our group of six volunteers. 'This is a syntropic farm,' explains one of them. 'That basically means we grow a whole lot of different food plants here to help restore the ecosystem, and we don't use chemicals to do that.' The aim of this kind of farming, she says, is to rejuvenate degraded soil and to create habitats rich in diversity of vegetation, wildlife and microorganisms. It's a truly reciprocal way of farming that gives as much as it takes, and that harnesses the regenerative power of earth. It's essentially about cooperating with nature, rather than fighting against it, as we so often do.

Soil health is the most important thing here, since soil can absorb and sequester huge amounts of greenhouse gases. If we can keep it healthy, it could be the very thing to help balance our climate, while also feeding the world. Pick up a handful of healthy soil, say the farmers, and you'll be holding more organisms than the number of people who've ever lived on Planet Earth.

We volunteers are given different jobs, and I'm on planting. I make my way over to a patch of earth where dozens of small rocket saplings are waiting to go into the ground. One of the farmers, a warm young woman named Lydia, shows me how to 'tickle' the saplings' root ball, teasing them out of the shape of their planters so they can spread out into the soil. She shows me the best way to water the new plants in, then leaves me to it. I drop to my knees and get to work.

The soil here is dark and rich and alive with worms and bugs. It smells sweet, and I have to resist the urge to push my face into it. I work, relishing the shade of the banana palms, watching butterflies and bees drifting in and out of the corn, feeling focused and alive. The edginess that has followed me intermittently for the past couple of years vanishes: I'm nowhere but here.

When it's time to leave, Lydia encourages us to harvest a basket of food and flowers to take home as payment. I pick a handful of beans, a few wonky eggplants, five yellow sunflowers and a cutting of tulsi basil to plant at home. On the drive home, with the produce sitting on the seat beside me, I feel richer than I have in a long time.

~

My lettuces are starting to grow, their bright green leaves curling up towards the sun. It's a small and simple thing, but it seems nothing short of a miracle that soon these plants I've nurtured will feed us and our friends. The tulsi cutting, which was really just a stick two weeks ago, is starting to grow tiny leaves. In my patch I've also added three marigold plants and two eggplant vines, and my chest swells with pride as I watch them grow.

Since the pandemic, when friends have told me how busy they are, I've felt a sense of creeping shame about not having much going on. I was always the one flitting around the world, either on an exotic trip or planning one, or meeting a tight deadline. There was always such strong momentum to my life, and I secretly loved being the one who always had the most interesting stories to tell at dinner parties and always had the most going on. I loved telling people what I did for a living; I loved being told I had the best job in the world; I loved that when people would compliment a piece of clothing I had on I could say, 'Oh, this? Just a little something I picked up on my last trip to India.' I realise now that what I did for a living was a source of great pride for me, the thing that made me feel different from other people, the thing that made me feel special.

There's a groundlessness I feel from not working much now, as I try to reimagine my career without much far-flung travel, and a slightly nauseating inkling that if I'm not the one with the glamorous job, then I'm not worth much to anyone. Intellectually, I know that inkling is untrue and that kind of thinking is the result of the evils of our capitalist society, but still, I feel it. I wonder if I am enough, just as I am. Stripped of the job title and the exciting plans, I wonder who 'I' even am now.

Lately, when friends ask me how I am, I want to say, 'Oh, you know, teetering on the precipice of total self-annihilation, poor and all at sea a lot of the time, feeling like everyone else is in a boat and I'm in the ocean, paddling like mad trying to keep up with them, wondering if I'll ever work or make money again, trying to find joy in the small things, trying to do better for Planet Earth, trying to plant some new seeds in my soul, trying to survive.' But I don't. What I have been telling them, though, is that I'm not busy, trying to be okay with that and letting go of the weird impulse to compete with their busyness. I have been trying to feel like I am enough. I'm actually relishing having time to do things like garden, relishing how abundant it makes me feel to tend plants instead of work, and I'm trying not to let shame ruin that.

~

Early one Wednesday afternoon, I'm sitting on the steps of our deck under a denim-blue sky in a T-shirt and undies. My back is pressed against the hot wooden house, as I watch an orange and black Wanderer butterfly pause on a palm frond, wings spread wide. *Isn't this more worthy of my time,* I think, *than sitting in a room all day, poking at a keyboard?* My travel-writing work is still virtually non-existent, but I have 'pivoted'. Now I'm writing stories about sustainability, running writing workshops and teaching private students. I'm still relying on government payments to fill in the gaps, though.

Today, as most days, I must quiet the conditioned response that each passing minute is a minute of productivity lost. A dollar floating by unearned, a story left unpitched, a workshop gone unorganised, social media content not created. I remember that although, or maybe *because,* the butterfly will live only a week or so, its only concerns are to sip nectar and mate and laze in the sun. I remember the fact I learned in primary school: that butterflies can't take flight unless they raise their body temperature first, which is the reason for their basking. I remember that for humans, too, there can be no lift-off without rest.

~

While I've been busy in the veggie patch, Pete has been planting trees. Lots of trees. Lemon and papaya trees so we'll have fruit, two lemon myrtles for tea, birds nest ferns and native kentia palms and other gorgeous things I don't yet know the names of.

I love watching him garden. He slips into the kind of mental cathedral that Dad always does in the garden, carefully tending the plants like they're his mates, clipping and feeding them, then standing back to admire his handiwork. Maybe we do all end up marrying our parents, after all.

The other day, Pete called me out to the garden to explain to me how he'd resuscitated a nectarine tree that had been toppled in a storm. A year ago, that kind of interruption would have really annoyed me. No time to talk about toppled trees, honey, I'm off to Antarctica next week. Now, though, I'd struggle to imagine anything more delightful. Today, he called me out of my office to show me a shovelful of soil he'd just dug up that had earthworms wriggling through it, then spent ten minutes explaining why worms are so important to soil health.

'They aerate it, see?' he said, pointing to the moist, chocolate-coloured earth around them. 'They're like tiny compost systems. They eat the beneficial bacteria and process it in their stomachs, so their poo becomes richer in nutrients than the soil itself. If the soil's good, you should be able to throw a shovel into it and come up with half-a-dozen earthworms.' How could I do anything but hug him, tight as I could? He reminds me, almost daily, to look down at the leaves and the bugs and the dirt, when my head is stuck in the clouds.

The story of our marriage will be held in this garden. It has already witnessed our dedication to each other and to the plants, our time and our love. It has seen our neglect, too, and our distraction. The garden is teaching us both big lessons, which I know will feed into the health of our relationship.

Patience is a big one. Now, when I feel the urge to run, I step into the garden and observe the small shifts happening there instead, to remind myself that everything does change in time. Surrender is another important one. I can feed and trim and coax these plants, but ultimately I'm not in control of them – or indeed my life, which is a kind of comfort.

Mostly, though, our garden is teaching me that I can't have it all. That in life, we must give up some things we love, in order to find other things we love, and maybe that's not such a bad thing. In giving up all the things I loved so dearly about foreign travel – the cultural stimulation, the constant education and inspiration, the excellent food and hotels, the excitement and freedom and novelty of it all – I have gained other things. Would I have tended this garden, our own habitat, so diligently if I was still whizzing around the globe a dozen times a year? Would I have tended my marriage in the way these months have allowed me to? Would I have taken the time to look more deeply at the land I was born on, to finally feel a sense of belonging to it and to the earth itself? I'm sure the answer is no. I close my eyes and listen to the sea crashing in the distance, to the butcher bird sending her song into the world, to my heart's steady rhythm. There, beneath it all, the whisper of peace.

~

Back on the farm, it's weeding time. The air is clear, and the light is luminous as we listen to Lydia talk about how great weeds are for soil conservation. This is important, since healthy soil sucks up carbon dioxide, but destroyed soil sends carbon back into the atmosphere. Destroyed soil also eventually turns to dust, leading to desertification, which sees about forty million people every year being pushed off their land.

The good news, says Lydia, is that weeds can help prevent desertification. They shade the soil surface, keeping it moist, and draw nutrients and water up from the deep soil and down from the air, making them more available for the plants around them. Weeds also tend to pop up in unhealthy soil, bringing it back into balance. When there are too many weeds, though, they suck too many nutrients out of the soil, making the surrounding plants suffer. Like everything in life, it's all about balance.

Lydia ushers me and a handsome volunteer with dark wavy hair and bright blue eyes over to a row of zucchinis that has been overtaken by weeds. While we crouch down to weed, we talk. The guy soon tells me he's here because he was addicted to methamphetamine and is looking for new hobbies to fill his sober life. He's renting and doesn't have a garden, but he grew up on land and misses having his hands in the soil. He asks about me, and I tell him my story, about wanting to assuage my eco-anxiety and atone for the sins of my carbon-heavy past, by looking for ways to come into deeper relationship with the land I've been running away from for a long time.

Most of the other volunteers I've met here are also searching for something. There's the bubbly English photographer who's dissatisfied with her work and looking for an out, and the woman who works with disadvantaged Indigenous kids and needs to de-stress. We're all here for more than gardening. We're here to build community with other plant lovers, to learn more about the land we're living on, to tend to plants so we can learn to better tend to ourselves.

I continue easing the rangy clumps out of the soil and piling them up behind me. It feels unusually satisfying to be clearing space for the other plants, to help resuscitate them in this way. Which is, I guess, what so many of us have been doing in our own lives over the past two years. Clearing time and space, bringing in more air and sunlight so we can grow and evolve.

When I was still madly travelling the globe, time was always in short supply. If I wasn't off on a travel assignment, I was tapping out stories while squeezing in meetings and catch-ups and planning the next adventure. I once heard my favourite travel writer, Pico Iyer, describe why he liked living in rural Japan in a doll's house apartment with no car or bike, no bedroom and a TV with no programs he could understand. Being free from distraction and complication, he said, meant every day looked like a clear meadow with nothing in it, stretching towards the mountains.

When I first heard that phrase, it beckoned to me. I wanted that spaciousness, almost as much as I wanted to see the world and everything in it. There was a time when it simply wasn't enough for me to have journeyed to fifty-six, eighty-two or even 114 countries in a lifetime. There were 196 of them, and until they had all been scoured, I refused to rest. I was a greedy traveller who had boxes to tick, gazillions of them, and never enough time in which to tick them. Now, though, I'm getting a glimpse of Pico's meadow, and I'd like to spend far more time in it.

By now, I've pulled my gardening gloves off. My skin and the earth's skin are touching, and my hands and nails are darkening with soil, which is flecked with white strands of mycelium. Earlier, Lydia told us about the mycelial network, a fungal information superhighway made up of long threads that branch out in every direction, which flourishes under every step we take. It has more threads than our brain has neural pathways and forms a gigantic underground web that shares messages and nutrients between trees through electrical pulses.

I recently learned the mind-boggling fact that we humans carry up to two-and-a-half kilograms of bacteria in our bodies. Today I imagine the bacteria in my body and the bacteria in the soil combining, each giving the other what it needs. It feels reciprocal and right, and I can almost feel my body humming with aliveness. I know that if the soil beneath my feet had been blasted with industrial chemicals, I wouldn't be feeling this way.

I move back over to planting – this time, some winged beans along a fence line. It's a tiny thing, planting something. Insignificant, some might say. But it kind of shifts your perspective on everything, especially when the land you're planting isn't your own. When you give something to the land, something you won't personally receive the benefits of, you start turning away from the extractive mindset we've had for so long. The mindset where we take and take without any reciprocation, and from which the climate breakdown has been born. Plants give us so much. They're what we build our houses from, what we make our clothes from, what we eat and where we derive so many of our medicines from. Yet how often do we think about that, and give gratitude for it all?

Planting these beans, though, is one tangible thing I can do to introduce myself to a more regenerative way of thinking. I plant some beans, I give the land a small gift, I start thinking about how I can give back to every place I visit. I push the seeds into the soil, and with them, a wish. *May this plant grow strong and luscious and feed hundreds of people for months and years to come.*

~

My tulsi is thriving. The bush is up to my knees now and seeing it every day brings me a disproportionate amount of joy. This Indian herb is also known as 'holy basil', and it's an important symbol that Hindus in India worship as a deity. Seeing it thriving in the veggie patch, between the eggplants and wild raspberries, makes the garden feel like a shrine. Which is exactly what it's starting to become.

I have nurtured this plant and now it is nurturing me. Every morning I harvest some tulsi, steeping the purple tinged leaves in hot water and thinking, as I sip, that this herb is helping my body cope with stress and my mind become clear. When I go to friends' houses, I bring a bunch of tulsi with me, so we can share some tea. I love how this garden, like all gardens, encourages us to give extra, how they encourage us not to hoard.

In that sense, too, our garden is a powerful teacher. I give extra from the garden, and it encourages me to give extra elsewhere in my life. I look through my cupboard and notice I'm hoarding clothes. I don't need twenty-five dresses and twenty-one pairs of pants and seventeen kimonos. Even though we've had less income coming into the household than ever before, I start gifting the excess to friends who I know will love certain pieces, and selling others on Gumtree. I put my beloved car – a ten-year-old white BMW convertible that I named Cindy – onto a car-sharing site, both to make some extra money and so other people can have as much fun in her as I do.

Because I'm growing my own food, I'm starting to think more about where all the food we eat comes from – another lesson from the garden. When we go to the farmers' market, I speak to the growers more, because I am growing too. In the supermarket, a place I'm going to less, I now look at where the chips or pasta or nuts I'm buying come from. I want to invest in food from this land, not food that's been shipped here from the other side of the world. I'm making different choices, and it feels good.

I've even started making paper, strange as that may seem. I bought a kit online, thinking I'd make a few sheets for a few cards, and now it has become a sort of compulsion. Each afternoon I rummage through the recycling for pieces of wastepaper. I rip them up, throw them into the blender, and whiz it up into a light brown mush. Adding the pulp to a vat of water, I pull the mould through and let the water drip off, then press the fresh paper onto absorbent cloth. Afterwards, I let it dry in the sun.

It's surprising how satisfying the process is. Tearing up old bills and newspapers and toilet-paper wrappers and junk mail and scrawled notes, and turning them into something beautiful and useful. It feels like childhood and kindergarten rooms. Like a protest against a world obsessed with waste. Like a kind of rescue mission.

When I look at my paper, with all its delicious quirks and imperfections, I see all the other lives it has lived. From tree to pulp to printing press to home to garbage bin and, now, to this. In an age of excess, the paper holds its own inherent power.

Sometimes, I add pollinator seeds to the pulp so that one day, if I'm feeling particularly brave, I can tear what I write to shreds, remembering that nothing is permanent, and plant my joys and my pains. I will hold on to nothing, transforming it all into new life: food for the birds and the bees.

~

When I notice the marigolds are struggling, that the vibrant orange flowers have become withered and brown, Pete teaches me about deadheading. The withered flowers need to be pulled off the plant, he says, to give new flowers a chance to grow. Otherwise, the plant keeps sending nutrients to the dead flowers, and there's not enough energy left for new growth. I pull the dead flowers off the bushes and am thrilled to find more than a dozen new flowers blooming just a few days later. It's a beautiful thing, to be able to help something grow, to be of service to something that cannot thank you with words. It makes me think about how this last couple of years have given me a chance to deadhead my own life. To pull off the parts that weren't working – the speed and constant movement, mostly – so I could channel energy into other areas and help them develop.

Tending our garden has helped me understand that I don't need magic mushrooms or anything else to hear plants speak to me. Pay enough attention to any living thing, and it will tell you what it needs. If the leaves of a plant are drooping, it's telling me it needs water. If a plant isn't growing, it's saying, *hey, I need more sunlight*. If I neglect my responsibilities, the garden will suffer, and it will start to neglect me.

Many of my friends have been reading a book called *Braiding Sweetgrass: indigenous wisdom, scientific knowledge and the teachings of plants*, written by the Indigenous botanist Robin Wall Kimmerer. It was published in 2013 but is only taking off in the mainstream now, a testament to how many of us have been pushed back into our neglected gardens. I've started reading it too, and soon I come across a sentiment that pretty much summarises everything I've been feeling about the relationship Pete and I are forming with our garden: 'Knowing that you love the earth changes you, activates you to defend and protect and celebrate. But when you feel that the earth loves you in return, that feeling transforms the relationship from a one-way street into a sacred bond.'

We *are* forming a sacred bond with our garden. Having a subtle conversation with it, and getting to know it and each other better every day because of that. I am becoming more curious about everything that existed here long before we moved in and started planting ourselves into this land, long before I was alive, even. I learn the names of each of the tall trees, the paperbarks and the eucalypts and the palms, that give us shade and air and life. I feel ashamed of how long it took me to say *hi, nice to meet you*, to these loyal friends and elders.

~

One afternoon I'm lying on the lawn, sunshine seeping through my skin and my blood and my bones. How many other human bodies have lain exactly where my body is now, I wonder. Hundreds of years ago, before there were houses and cars here, the Arakwal Indigenous people of this area would have been here, respecting this land as the living entity it is. Never taking more than was necessary. Always giving as they took.

In my mind's eye I see those people, the rightful owners of this land, being pushed off it, then houses being erected in their place. I see land being divided up, fences being built, and white-skinned people like me moving in, thinking that because they've paid money to be here, they belong. I think about how I'm complicit in all of this, and how the very least I can do by way of apology is to give back to the wild, entangled web of life beneath my feet. To be the best caretaker I can be, for everyone who tended this land in the past and who will live on it in the future. None of them will know a thing about what happened in this garden to keep it alive. None of them will know that this garden is where one woman learned, by putting some plant roots into the earth, how to put her own roots into the earth too.

6

Coral

Road tripping to the Great Barrier Reef

Standing inside a cold white steel shed on a farm in the Noosa hinterland, a four-hour drive from home, I'm holding a mushroom the size of my head in my hands. Not a magic mushroom, this time, but an oyster mushroom – delicate, coral pink and blooming upwards so its ruffled underbelly shows.

I'm here with a thirty-something guy with kind blue eyes named Scott, who quit his job in oil and gas to start farming mushrooms. For the past half-hour he's been telling me how these mushrooms can be used to break down petrochemicals, absorb radiation from contaminated soil and water, and even heal our bodies and brains by creating new neural pathways. As he's been talking, we've been walking around admiring the mushrooms, which are spawning from the sides of their grow-out bags: tongues of thick, blue-tinged oyster caps; hairy white lion's manes that look like bulbous throbbing brains; clusters of canary-yellow oyster mushrooms.

How did I get here? Well, a few weeks after the psilocybin journey, I started feeling that familiar sense of dread sweeping over me again. I felt plugged into my surroundings, very much so, and the natural world around me definitely seemed more vibrant and alive. But with no one able to travel beyond Australia, the socialising in our town was at an all-time high, and life quickly started feeling claustrophobic again. In a single day there could be invitations to a beach picnic, a walk, a dinner, drinks and dancing. Which might all sound lovely, but I felt like a boxer thrusting my gloves up in front of my face, trying to fend them all off.

In The Before, when I was away all the time, I missed a lot of this socialising, which was something I was mostly glad about. I'd always rather be off exploring interesting places and learning new things than seeing the same people week after week, talking about the same things. Now, though, my time didn't feel like it was my own, and I started feeling a desperate urge to get out. I came upon Katherine Mansfield's words in the Nikki Gemmell book I was reading: 'I feel a real horror of people closing over me.' I thought, that's exactly it.

I recently discovered, thanks to Susan Cain's wonderful 2012 book *Quiet: the power of introverts in a world that can't stop talking*, that I am a classic 'introverted extrovert'. An outgoing introvert, who can be the life of the party in social situations, but who also finds that very draining and needs lots of alone time to recharge. I love being with people, but only sometimes, and mostly for short periods. Ever since I was small I have relished my own company – reading, thinking, writing, walking alone in nature – and find that these are the best ways I can imagine to spend time. One of the things I liked best about travel writing was that it presented the perfect landscape to be my 'ambivert' self. I could be out in the world seeing new and different things and socialising with new and different people, then tuck myself away in my room for hours at a time to reflect and write about it all.

Now that lockdown was over, I didn't want to be sitting in cafes, gossiping about other people and real estate, and going to endless lunches and parties. I wanted to be out bushwalking, sleeping under the stars, reading and writing and processing all these seismic changes we had all been going through. I wanted to see interesting places and meet passionate people who were doing something about the mess we were in. I found myself constantly wondering why everyone was staying so insanely sanguine, while I felt as though I was losing my mind. *We're breaking the planet!* I felt like shouting whenever I was walking down the street. *Why don't you care?*

A few weeks earlier I'd gone to a friend's glitzy party at his beautiful house in the hinterland above where we live. I'd been excited about it, but once I got there, I felt oddly hollow and like I was performing in some kind of pantomime. After the horror of the fires and the pandemic and all the death and destruction that came in their wake, it didn't feel right to be dancing and clinking champagne. I was wearing a dress printed with illustrations of endangered species, and I started cornering people and quietly evangelising to them about how dire the situation was for the whales and leopards and rhinos and armadillos and snakes printed on my outfit. I knew, even as I was doing it, that I needed a fresh perspective.

And so, last minute, I decided to take a road trip to the Daintree rainforest. It was a 2000-kilometre drive that would take me about two weeks each way, and one I'd do completely on my own. I needed my blinkers to be off, and I deeply missed the feeling of anonymity I used to experience when I'd head off on assignments alone. I missed the feeling of being completely myself, free of the judgements of people who wanted me to be the version of me that fitted for them. Travel always provided the perfect escape. The anonymity of the road was the medicine I needed.

Aside from getting away from everything, I was going for professional reasons, too. Over the past year I'd been working on a book called *Go Lightly: how to travel without hurting the planet,* about how to travel more sustainably, the topic that had been obsessing me ever since returning from the Arctic. The book covered topics including travelling less but better, putting nature at the centre of our travels, supporting locally owned businesses, giving back to local communities and more. It would be hitting bookshelves in a couple of months, and I wanted to get out there and do all the things I espoused in the book – hiking, boating, camping and connecting with sustainably minded businesses – before it did. I wanted to stay accountable.

While lots of my friends baulked at me going alone, Pete was nothing but supportive. This has always been his way – to lead with kindness and love, not jealousy and restriction. He wants me to be who I am, and to have the life I want, which means that in the past he almost always supported me heading off to Papua New Guinea or Borneo or wherever work was taking me. He always says he misses me, but he never makes me feel bad for needing what I need. He wants me to live my life without guard rails, because that's what he wants, too. And I know he knows better than I do that the way we thrive in a relationship is by supporting each other's dreams and growth, not pushing each other's heads under water.

~

The Noosa hinterland was the first stop on my itinerary, and I've spent my first two days staying in a turmeric-coloured rammed-earth lodge set high on a hill, visiting a permaculture farm, kayaking through the Everglades, meeting Scott and his mushrooms, and generally just throwing myself back into the world with all the gusto of a cooped-up travel writer. When I pull out of Scott's driveway, though, I have butterflies in my stomach. The real journey is only just beginning.

As I drive through the hot afternoon, three and a half hours north of Noosa and bound for the small seaside town of Miara, fear starts to tiptoe in. I wonder whether my friends were right. Was it really a good idea for me to do this alone?

I spent so much of my early life letting fear lead the way. I was the kid who didn't want to swim because the water was too cold, or the waves were too big, who didn't want to climb because the tree was too high, who didn't want to ski because she might fall. I remember visiting a farm with my family when I was about six and getting stuck at the top of a hill because there were cows in the field next to the path I was following

– behind a fence, mind you, but what if they figured out how to jump over it and trampled me? At thirteen, when I was off sick from school, my friends signed me up for surfing lessons as a practical joke, knowing how deathly afraid I was of the ocean. I made excuses every single week for the rest of term – I forgot my bathers, had my period, hurt my foot – and only had to get in the water once. I shielded myself for so long that I taught myself how to be afraid.

That's why, when I started travelling for a living, I made myself put my hand up for assignments that scared me. I didn't want to stick with that first draft of my life story. Knowing that wrapping myself up in cotton wool wasn't the answer, I wanted to go to remote places like Mongolia and Papua New Guinea, where I would be forced to do terrifying things like fly in small planes and climb active volcanoes and abseil off cliffs. Cotton wool would keep the danger and the fear out, sure, but it would also keep out the brave, open-hearted life I dreamt of living. I wanted more than anything to be courageous because I knew that the braver I was, the better life became.

I crack the window and taste the diesel smoke, acid and oily, belching out of the truck in front of me. As the bitter odour sinks into my gut, I turn my mind away from thoughts of fear and towards the conversation I had with the permaculture farmer I visited yesterday. As we walked through his overgrown property, where lettuce and beans, dragon fruit and strawberries grew wild amongst the weeds, he told me a story. During the Edo period in Japan, when a child was born the parents would plant some trees, and when that child married, the trees would be cut to build their house. 'Imagine what kind of world we'd be living in now, if we all still thought that way?' he'd said, as he pulled some kale leaves off a plant for me to take home for my dinner.

I can hardly imagine it, living in this light-speed, over-consumptive world, where clothes and furniture and cars are built with planned obsolescence in mind so that we're caught in an endless cycle of consumption. But a world in which we all thought like Edo-period families is exactly the kind of self-sustaining, forward-thinking world I want to live in – one where we're all responsible for creating as many of our own resources as possible.

My mind rolls around like this until I finally reach Miara. My chosen spot for the night is in as unglamorous a town as you could imagine, popular with fishermen and with only thirty-eight people living in it. But it is also set on the banks of a pretty river lined with mangroves, the campground isn't overrun, and it feels simple in a way that takes me back to my childhood.

I drive up to my campsite, set under a huge casuarina and about 5 metres away from the river, and immediately head out for a walk along the deserted mudflats. The sun is low, the shadows are long, and I walk barefoot along the cool, wet sand without seeing another soul. With my mind clear from the day's driving, and without someone by my side to distract me, I start to notice everything around me: the luscious mangroves reaching out towards the water, the salt-bleached tree boughs washed up against the shore.

My eyes drop down and land on the millions of tiny balls of sand arranged on the low tide into abstract patterns. I focus in on these fascinating natural artworks. I recently found out they are created by sand bubbler crabs, found only here in northern Australia. The blue-and-white crabs, only about a centimetre wide, gather sand into their mouths, turning it over into balls as they search for tiny bits of organic matter to eat. When they're done, they spit the sand balls out and kick them aside, making the enchanting patterns I'm looking at now, which radiate outwards about a metre from their burrows.

Soon, I start to see hundreds of these crabs, scuttling along in groups of a few dozen. When I get close, I watch in amazement as they all suddenly bury themselves. I squat down on the sand close to one crab and watch it spin around in a circle at breakneck speed, pulling sand up over its head with its claws until nothing is left but a little mound of sand.

I get it, I think. *I know exactly how that is.* Sometimes you do just need to escape everything and hide away to replenish yourself before returning to the brightness of the world. I guess that's what this solo trip, and all the solo trips before it, were all about.

Back at camp, I head over to the outdoor barbecue and make myself some rice noodles with spinach and Scott's mushrooms, which I eat sitting on the grass, straight from the pot. At dusk, I take a quick hot shower in the communal bathroom and settle into bed in the back of Gloria. Gloria is Pete's car, which I've taken on this trip because mine was too small. He called her Gloria because he thinks she's an old lady's car, a white Prius that used to belong to a pathology lab. 'Bed' is a narrow single mattress, covered with a single sheet and the poncho Pete's mum gave him, which he wanted me to take on this trip. I crack the back windows open, pull the boot door closed, click on the fairy lights I brought with me, knowing they'd liven up most dire situations, and settle in to read my book.

As I lie there, I think about how far this is from the glamorous life I was leading not so long ago. Almost two years ago to the day I was in the Maldives reviewing a resort for work, staying in an elegant overwater villa that cost more than $1600 a night. I spent my time there drinking Ruinart champagne and diving off my deck into that famously clear, bath-warm water, taking guided snorkelling trips and sundown dolphin-watching cruises over the UNESCO Biosphere Reserve reef it was set on, having massages in the spa, and occasionally calling my attentive 'island host' – otherwise known as a butler – for a fresh coconut. It was fabulous, all right, even when I got terrible diarrhoea on day two. But it was also kind of empty. My schedule meant I didn't even leave the resort, and to this day I can tell you very few things about Maldivian culture. Tonight, as I fall asleep to the sound of the lake lapping gently against the sand, with the light of the moon spilling onto my bed, I'm grateful that life has led me here. Back to basics, where everything superfluous has been stripped away.

~

My newfound appreciation for simplicity does, however, have its limits. I discover this the next day when I board the catamaran I'm going to spend the next two nights on, with eight travellers I've never met, and discover my 'bedroom' is in fact the couch in the middle of the lounge room. You know, like a stretch of banquette seating that's right next to the dining table where everyone will hang out.

Luckily, hanging out inside the boat is not what I'm here for. I'm here to explore the Great Barrier Reef, a place I last came to thirty years ago. I'm excited to get out there, but also nervous. Half the coral on the reef has been lost since 1995, because of rising global temperatures, but also because of dynamite fishing, cyclones and crown-of-thorns starfish. I wonder if all I'll see out there are coral graveyards.

As soon as we start motoring away from shore, I head up to the bow to look out over the water, blue-green despite a heavy blanket of cloud, and feel the crisp ocean breeze on my skin. When darkness falls, we eat a simple pasta salad dinner on the lower deck, then sit on the side of the boat and watch dozens of reef sharks feed. As the sharks swoop through the soft blue lights emitted by the boat, I think about how they've been living here for millions of years, and how we're newcomers to their backyard. I think about them and all the biodiversity we're set to lose on Earth. If we continue business as usual, we and these sharks are going to be in real trouble, because our fate and the ocean's are one and the same. Scientists say 50 to 80 per cent of the oxygen we breathe is generated by the ocean, and it absorbs a big chunk of our carbon emissions – about six times the amount released by cars around the world. Without a healthy ocean, there is no healthy us. There is nothing on this earth that isn't connected. This isn't just something the mushrooms taught me. It's something almost every journey I've ever been on has taught me.

My thoughts drift back to one of those journeys, to Ethiopia three years ago, where I took Pete on a surprise fortieth birthday trip. We love Ethiopian jazz, and I was eager to see it performed in the place it originated, as well as spend an Orthodox Christmas at the rock-cut churches of Lalibela.

Two hundred thousand pilgrims descended on Lalibela that year. In the late afternoon of Ethiopian Christmas Day, we arrived in the midst of all those pilgrims, at the rock-hewn churches that had been cut nine stories into the earth nine hundred years before by a king who claimed angels had helped him build them overnight. Pilgrims were everywhere, pressing through the cobbled streets, wrapped in gauzy white Ethiopian cotton and sitting on the dusty earth tending fires and cooking food. Clouds of frankincense shifted through the air along with the smell of coffee.

Soon night fell, and the frosted sea of humanity slowly rolled over the churches, slipping down into them as the Christmas ceremonies began. Five hundred priests clad in embroidered, bejewelled robes and brandishing intricate silver Orthodox crosses chanted their sermons down below, as we sat on the 12-metre cliffs surrounding the churches.

All around us, the pilgrims swayed their bodies back and forth as they chanted, hunched over their bibles, their faces aglow with candlelight. One woman to our right started convulsing, her body becoming an earthquake, while two worried friends gathered around her. A priest arrived and started whispering incantations over the woman, tapping his bible on her forehead and flicking holy water over her with his fingers. Drawing her back from the demon that had entered her.

It's difficult to explain, but whatever entered the woman then somehow wafted over and pervaded my own body. Twenty minutes later my stomach started mirroring her convulsing body. I pushed, sweating and shaking through the dark, upstream through the crowds, to the single bathroom. As I sat there, letting the wave rush through me, I thought about the interconnectedness of all of us. I was that woman. I was her demons. I was her angels too. My body was her body, my spirit her spirit. There is no separation, I knew then. It is something the world tells us, over and over again, if only we stop to listen.

I head back up from the lower deck to my boat-couch bed. I pull on my eye mask and shove some wet toilet paper into my ears to drown out the sound of the couple happily drinking rum and playing cards at the table right next to me. I fall asleep with a head full of sea.

~

The next two days are full of nature. We hike through lush bush to a point overlooking Whitehaven, Australia's most photographed beach, with its famously white silica sand and aquamarine water. We walk down to the beach to swim with manta rays, then spend the afternoon snorkelling, watching fish as large as dinner platters swirling all around us. We paddleboard around an almost-deserted cove, then go for a sail while a pod of dolphins plays at the front of the boat.

It is blissful, but it is also sad. Sad because the reason those big fish were there while we snorkelled was because our captain was feeding them. Sad because most of the coral I saw was dead, covered in light brown algae and nothing like the technicolour coral beds I remember from my childhood. Sad because the rising sea temperatures causing this reef degradation can be partially attributed to oil-powered boats, just like the one I'm on. Sad because when our skipper pulled the anchor up to go for that sail, a big chunk of coral came up with it.

And yet, as I lie on the top deck while we motor back to shore, I look down at the reef, home to more than 1600 species of fish and one-third of the world's soft coral, and think how important it is to see all of it: the beauty and the devastation. It's important because once you see it, you understand unequivocally what's at stake, and you become an ambassador for it. As the deep ecologist and Buddhist scholar Joanna Macy wrote in a 2020 op-ed for *Emergence Magazine* called 'Entering the Bardo', 'When we dare to face the cruel social and ecological realities we have been accustomed to, courage is born and powers within us are liberated to reimagine and even, perhaps one day, rebuild a world.'

So while I'm deflated, I'm also activated. I know that for every devastated stretch of reef, there's one that is pristine and teeming with the kind of life we see in David Attenborough documentaries – orange-and-white striped clownfish playing hide-and-seek in the fronds of anemones, schools of black manta rays gliding through the water, violet, lime and magenta corals covering the seabed, as lumpy as oversized brains, or as delicate as French lace. While I didn't see these abundant reef sections on this trip, I know they are there and that we must celebrate them. Not in order to pull the wool over our eyes, but to help us fall in love with this place, so we'll go home and do everything we can to protect it.

7

Rainforest

Facing fear in the Daintree

It's getting dark when the owner of the Daintree campground I'm staying in, a thin guy in his sixties with watery blue eyes and mottled skin, starts telling me how police rarely come to this part of the Daintree rainforest. It's too hard to cross the river, he says. Then he proceeds to tell me how he and his mates once beat up a misbehaving traveller and dumped his unconscious body at the ferry at dawn. I titter nervously, a little rattled.

He peers at me through the gloaming and says, 'You know, when I heard a journalist was coming and then *you* showed up, I thought, *phwoar!* I could hardly speak! I wasn't expecting someone who looked like you.'

Okay, I think, *I'm out.*

When he suggested we have a beer an hour ago, I said yes, thinking nothing more of it than *I'm sure this guy has a few great tales to tell.* Which he absolutely did. He and his wife, who's away for the week, live in an old bus, and we've been sitting on the concrete patio out front in the dying light. He's been telling me rollicking tales about how he used to be a judo instructor in a past life, about how he skippered a boat on the Great Barrier Reef for years, about what it's like living deep in the oldest intact rainforest in the world.

Now, though, I tell him I should go – that it's time for dinner and I should be getting back to my campsite. I stand and walk out onto the driveway, and he follows me.

'Stay for dinner,' he says, 'I have some fish.' Pause. 'I'd *really* like you to stay for dinner.' When I say no thanks, I need to go, he puts his hand on my forearm, raises his eyebrows and says, 'You can ... stay here tonight? Please, I'd *really* like you to stay.'

I start to quietly panic, energy zigzagging up my legs and into my chest and arms. A minute ago, I was feeling a little hazy from two beers, but now everything is as sharp as crocodile's teeth. Aside from one other couple, and who knows where they are in this campground, there's no one here. I'm in the middle of the Daintree rainforest, even Pete doesn't know exactly where I am, and this guy's just told me that the police don't come here.

A million thoughts crash through my brain while the blood rushes to my head, roaring in my ears, and my heart starts hammering hard in my chest.

'No, really, thanks, but I have ... plenty to eat. I should really go,' I stammer, as I pull my arm away and walk fast as I can up the pathway towards my car. My footsteps crunching on the gravel ring out into the night, disproportionately loud. 'Goodnight!' I yell over my shoulder as I break into a trot, trying to sound nonchalant. 'See you tomorrow!'

I do not want to piss this guy off.

I get back to the car, fumbling with the keys as I unlock it, and climb into the back, locking the doors behind me. I haven't had dinner, I haven't showered or brushed my teeth, but I'm way too scared to go back outside now. What if he's waiting for me out there? *Just breathe.* I'm staying on his land. He could feel entitled and hurt and he could be getting drunk and he could be down there scheming and he could be on his way up to me right now. *Just breathe.* How could I have been so naive? To think I could come out here on my own and have a drink with that guy and that he wouldn't think anything of it? To think that just because he's much closer to my dad's age than mine that he wouldn't try something? *Just breathe.*

For the past few days in the rainforest, I've had moments of fear about crocodiles and snakes and cassowaries. But, as it turns out, the animal I most had to fear was another human. We are the most dangerous creatures on Earth. I lie awake for hours, cramped and hot. I want to open the windows, but I'm too afraid. I try to imagine the earth beneath me, holding me and rocking me to sleep. I sometimes do this when I have trouble sleeping, remembering that the earth is always there to support me and hold me. But tonight it's not working. Tonight I do not feel held by anything. Tonight there is nothing that can help me feel safe.

~

When I arrived in the Daintree three days ago, I did feel safe. Strong and capable, after the long drive there from the Great Barrier Reef, and the much longer drive there from home that some people had thought I couldn't or shouldn't do alone. Because the campsite I'd booked was across the Daintree River, I'd had to drive Gloria onto a car ferry to get there, which didn't freak me out in the slightest at the time. As I drove down the single-lane road covered over by rainforest, palms and ancient fig trees, I was excited by the remoteness, the feeling of entering a last frontier.

I pulled into my campsite, set on a vast sprawling lawn surrounded by thick rainforest, and found my undercover spot. It was wet season, the time most visitors carefully avoid, and also mid-pandemic, so there were only a couple of other vehicles parked across the campground. I'd been loving the quietude everywhere else so far, but being solo in the rainforest suddenly felt a little daunting. Something about the immensity of it, or the prehistoric feeling of the place, maybe. I couldn't quite put my finger on it.

~

When I was a kid, I loved tiny things. I had a three-centimetre-squared notebook with a pink marbled cover that was my first journal, and a set of miniature coloured pencils that were so precious to me I could barely bring myself to use them. My favourite miniature things, though, were in the garden. I'd spend hours out there, capturing ants for my ant farm and watching them create mazes in the sand, and examining the smallest flowers with a magnifying glass. My best friend and I had matching bug catchers and would pick ladybugs off the trees to fill them with. I once found tiny lizard eggs in the garden and sat on the steps next to them for hours in the midday sun, waiting for them to hatch.

By high school, my passion for friends and boys and study overtook my passion for tiny creatures, then the warp-speed work world obliterated it, like a total eclipse of the sun. The world in my computer became far more important than the natural world. Then, when I started travelling at fever pitch, I simply didn't have time to stop and stare at the little things that had once fascinated me. Since life has slowed down, though, I have felt that acute focus I had as a kid returning.

I noticed that old focus when I was out hiking the next morning, following a wooden boardwalk through the rainforest as a light rain sifted down around me. I passed a spider's web and stopped to watch the orb spider at work, marvelling at how this creature pulls elastic silk out of her body with her legs, silk that's stronger than steel, and weaves a perfect web with it. I peered at a spiny pandanus palm leaf and was amazed to find a peppermint stick insect tucked into its fold, camouflaged against predators. Once I'd seen one, I saw dozens. Then I looked up and saw a blazing blue Ulysses butterfly drifting through the trees. I felt as though the forest was pouring itself into me, reminding me of all the things we humans are missing as we speed through life.

I was still feeling a sense of eeriness being out in the rainforest alone, though. I put it down to the constant rain, to the constant signs warning me of lurking crocodiles. Craving both company and the deeper story of the land, I jumped on my phone and signed up for a tour with a local

Kuku Yalanji Aboriginal man named Juan Walker, who picked me up the next day in a minibus and drove me and two other travellers to the furthest reaches of Cape Tribulation.

We followed Juan's dreadlocked head down the rainforest paths, the dappled light flickering as he pointed out the wait-a-while palm's barbed tendrils, which his ancestors used to cut meat and hook fish, and the sarsaparilla leaves that are used as soap. Juan led us to a deserted beach where we stood beneath purple storm clouds, a safe 5 metres from the water's edge to avoid crocs. He plucked a handful of thin casuarina twigs off a tree, and told us that when they're heated, they're a salve for twisted ankles and swollen knees. Then he pointed out the prop roots of the mangroves, where the mud crabs his people eat are found, but he emphasised that they never take more crabs than they need. Everything relies on everything else, he said. If one thing disappears, everything else is affected, so always give back to the land as you take and make sure there's enough for future generations. You have to look after Mother Nature, he said, or she won't look after you.

The idea echoed in my mind later when I went swimming with a woman I met on the tour, also travelling alone, in a waterhole the colour of jade. We walked through the forest, the rain dripping through the thick palms, cycads, soaring figs and twisting vines, surrounded by the rush of the river and the pop and crackle of insects. At the river, we stripped off and threw our naked bodies into the crisp water, so clear I could see the ancient boulders sitting far below the surface. My body filled with its green, my blood filled with its cold. Lying on my back, I let the water hold me, and fancied I could almost hear the wild, ancient conversation going on between the water, the granite and the forest. I felt completely fearless. In that moment, I really did believe that nature would look after me.

~

The morning after the incident with the campground owner, I leave the Daintree at dawn. I've barely slept, but I know the driving will be good for my jangled nerves. I put on a playlist Pete made me specifically for the trip, wind the windows down and inhale big lungfuls of forest air, and begin my long journey home. It feels impossibly far away right now.

The more road I put between me and the rainforest, the more I feel my fear and self-flagellation dissolve and transform. My palms start to get slick against the wheel, and I can feel heat prickling in my cheeks. How dare that guy try that on me, knowing he was in a position of power. How dare he make me feel unsafe, knowing I was alone and vulnerable. How dare he make me question whether I shouldn't have travelled on my own, when doing that feels like the thing that's saving me right now.

My entire adult life, I've railed against the idea that women aren't capable of doing everything men can do. I went to an all-girls' selective high school that pushed us to think critically and drilled into us the message that we could be prime ministers or surgeons or lawyers or anything we wanted to be. Part of the reason I wanted to become a travel journalist was that, after reading so many books written mostly by older white men like Paul Theroux or William Dalrymple, I wanted to fearlessly explore the world and prove that women could just as easily do it too. Part of the reason I married Pete was that he's a feminist who never forces me into conventional female roles, who never questions my desire to do 'dangerous' things that no one would ever baulk at a man doing. And now, a complete stranger has made me question it myself.

My mind feels like a snow globe that's been turned upside down and shaken all around. I crank up the music and sing at the top of my lungs to blow off some steam for a good hour or two. By the time I pull into Paronella Park, the snow in my head has finally settled, and I'm much calmer.

When a friend told me there was an abandoned Spanish castle in the rainforest in Queensland that I just had to visit on this road trip, I thought, *Surely that can't be right. Surely I would have heard of it.* But I hadn't, and now here it is: a huge stone castle, covered in moss and being slowly overtaken by the forest, set beside a thundering waterfall. It's an eerily beautiful reminder of what happens when humans step back and let nature reclaim what was once hers.

It's getting dark as I wander through the castle grounds, and there's barely another soul in sight. I walk into one of the buildings, trailing my fingers across its damp, dilapidated walls and listening to the crash of the waterfall, especially loud after the recent rains. The brochure I picked up at reception tells me a Spanish guy named José Paronella built this place back in the 1930s. He made lots of money setting up and selling cane farms in the 1920s and decided to use it to bring his dream to life. Despite everyone telling him he was completely mad for doing it, he went ahead and built his castle with tennis courts, an ice-creamery, a theatre and a ballroom, for his family and the public to enjoy.

Walking through what remains of the abandoned castle, I'm in disbelief that a place like this exists in Australia. I look up at the mossy turrets and think, *Thank God for people like José, who silence the critics and fearlessly bring to life the magic they want to see in the world. Thank God for those inner voices that encourage all of us to live our dreams, no matter how strange they might seem to others.*

I sit on a low stone wall overlooking what once would have been the ballroom, and I make a decision. I will continue to find my wild, even if it means confronting danger, because I refuse to armour myself against life or let fear corrode my spirit. I will continue searching for beautiful things and places that fill me with astonishment, because it is the only thing that resuscitates me when I've lost my breath. And because I know that if the planet needs anything, it is people who are mischievous and unafraid and full of awe – people who are free.

Part Two

Awakening

8

Rock

Feeling soliphilia in the bush

One of my closest friends, Amy, gives me a book as a gift. She's as neurotic and sensitive as I am, and so knows that a climate crisis book is as close to a perfect gift as I could imagine. It's called *The Future We Choose,* written by Christiana Figueres and Tom Rivett-Carnac, the leaders of negotiations on the 2015 Paris Agreement global climate pact. One quiet, stormy Sunday morning at home, I read a statistic that floors me. Only 6 per cent of the world's population has ever set foot on a plane. Six per cent! I have to read it three times before I can properly absorb it.

The authors have a message for those of us in that very privileged 6 per cent. They write that we should dramatically reduce the number of flights we take – to take the train instead, or limit flights to a certain number per year, or choose video conferencing over in-person meetings. I still need to read these kinds of things often. I need to be reminded, as someone who travels for a living, that it's my duty to do things better.

Before there is no beautiful world left to see. I need to be reminded because I am still finding not jumping on a plane and running away to faraway places very difficult.

I'm beginning to think that this difficulty has to do with something else I read about in *The Future We Choose*. It's called the South Indian monkey trap, a cruel device made out of a coconut with a hole in it and a ball of rice inside. Monkeys squish their hand in to grab the rice, but the hole isn't big enough for their clenched fist to come back through. If the monkeys let go of the rice, they'd be free. But they don't. They're trapped by their desire.

This, says the book, is how we are as modern humans. We buy, we use, we experience, we discard. Over and over, knowing we're trapped, but being so addicted to the cycle that we can't let go. We know that what we're doing is causing the fires and floods and droughts that are decimating Earth, but at the same time we want desperately to affirm our identities through the experiences and possessions that advertising and social media promise will improve our lives. Our lives, which are already full of so much beauty and magic, but we cannot see it for all the stuff piling up around us.

I think about how I'm still clinging to my old life and the way it's working like the South Indian monkey trap. Because I'm still clinging to travel, because my eye is still focused on the horizon, I'm desensitising myself to the beauty that is right beside me. I mean, how can these sedentary days in our sleepy beachside suburb feel special when I'm comparing them to adventuring on an icebreaker in Antarctica, or bumping through India in a rickshaw? The simple answer is that they can't.

These months of grounding down at home are, however, helping to re-sensitise me to the subtleties of life, and shift the idea of what a good life is. Ever so slowly, I'm beginning to loosen my grip on the ball of rice. Eventually, I may be able to pull my fist out of the coconut and make better choices.

These months have also been helping me to sit with the big questions I was running from for such a long time. Who am I beyond the glamorous job title? What responsibilities do I now hold as a human being living on an ailing planet? Why can't I seem to find the illumination I always sought from travel right here at home?

I still don't know the answers. But I am trying to find them. In days that are flat and stuffy, when I can't even remember what goosebumps felt like on my skin. And in days that are blissful in their simplicity, when I understand life was never meant to be a string of ecstatic highs anyway.

Not that my travelling life was always that rosy. I need to remember that, too. I once got so sick in Nepal that my nose swelled up to twice its usual size and weeping sores popped up all over my face. I was staying in a Buddhist retreat without any mirrors at the time, so I didn't realise how bad it was or how horrific I looked until I went to review a fancy hotel in the outskirts of Kathmandu. The elegant owner, who looked like a Nepali version of Sade and walked around with a long cigarette holder, actually retracted her hand from me and stepped back a metre when we were introduced at cocktail hour. When I got back home to Mumbai, where we were living at the time, I discovered I had an acute viral infection and was given a shot of steroids in my bottom, three sets of antibiotics, and strict instructions to not leave our apartment for two weeks.

Then there was that time in Morocco when I got such bad diarrhoea that I had to stuff myself full of Imodium so I could ride a donkey into the Atlas Mountains for the day. When my friend and I got back to the hotel, I promptly pooed my pants. There was that time in Israel when I left my passport in the hotel's photocopying machine and didn't realise until two days later when I was already halfway across the country, about to cross the border to Jordan, and Pete and I had to drive all the way back to get it. There was that trip to central Japan when I got terrible jet-lag-induced insomnia for days on end and a debilitating migraine with it, and used an inordinate amount of coffee and alcohol and painkillers to try to mask it until I could get home.

The point is, some of travelling life was horrendously, crushingly, gruesomely awful. The larger point is, I don't want to wish any of the days of my life away. Not the awful ones, not the bland ones, either. What a terrible waste. And so today, as for the past five hundred–plus days since I last set foot on a plane overseas, I make myself a promise. I will practise keeping my eyes as alert for those goosebump-inducing moments here as they were in those distant lands.

I put the book down and ask Pete to play *bagh-chal* with me. It's a board game we bought in Nepal, where one player controls four tigers that 'hunt' the other player's twenty goats. I always hated board games, didn't understand the point of them, but this brass board and its mini figurines was so pretty it drew me in. Now I'm hooked. We sit on the floor and start playing, while Milka curls up and falls asleep beside us. We sip our coffee, the washing machine whirrs in the background and we move the little brass tigers and goats across the board.

I am inching closer to loving the poetry of our dailiness. And maybe this – this learning to be still and at home with each other – really is just another kind of great adventure.

Our love is truer now than it has ever been. There are fewer wild journeys, but more rambling conversations, more mornings wandering empty beaches and nights spent wrapped in each other's arms by the fire. Less chasing, and more simply allowing things to unfold, whatever that looks like at the time.

And maybe this is the real secret: this acceptance of the fact that we're forever going to be leaving behind past versions of ourselves and our marriage as we uncurl and blossom. We are learning that attempting to cling to a past that no longer exists is only going to cause pain.

I don't want to waste precious time in pointless competition with the past. What a way to ruin the beauty of the present moment. What a way to miss the entrance into the next, possibly more beautiful and truer, iteration of our life, faintly pulsing like a heartbeat beneath it all. Pete laughs as he takes one of my goats off the board, and I never want the game to end.

~

I've started wondering where this constant search for novelty and extraordinary experiences came from in me. I definitely wasn't brought up like that. In fact, I had the most stable upbringing you could imagine. My parents bought into a nice area on Sydney's north shore when it wasn't nice, stayed until it became nice, and they're still there more than fifty years later. Mum worked as a schoolteacher and Dad worked three jobs to pay the mortgage, which is noble and beautiful and good, and I appreciate it all more than they might ever know. Mum made sure there was consistency behind everything my sister and I did, which is also noble and beautiful and good. We both played piano and another instrument – me violin, my sister flute – and she made sure we practised an hour every day, made sure we ate well and studied hard and were immersed in art and culture. We went to good schools; Mum and Dad never fought; it was all very safe and secure.

But I suppose that's what I became afraid of. Because at a certain point I decided that I didn't want to stay safe. I wanted my life to be bigger and more expansive than that. I wanted it to be explosive.

When I dreamt of my future, I didn't dream of safety – of marriage and babies and houses. I dreamt of meeting tribes in Africa, of soaking in hot springs in Japan, of meeting holy men at festivals in India. And when those dreams finally became a reality, I clutched them tight to my chest and vowed never to let them go.

~

There's a personality test called the Enneagram that I discover in a book by one of my favourite Buddhist teachers, Susan Piver. It describes patterns in how we interpret the world and manage emotions, and is broken down into nine types. When I read the description for type number four, I think, *My God, that's me.*

'While others may prize ordinariness – *I just want my life to be normal* – for this person, to be "normal" is a sign of failure. When one's avoidance is of the ordinary, there is a constant, often agitated search for what else is possible because whatever you actually see, do, or acquire immediately becomes ordinary by virtue of possessing it.'

A lot of my life I have been searching, in an itchy, dissatisfied kind of way, for new experiences and people and places. The more I've seen, the more I've wanted to see. I wanted to fill myself with the world. I became what Buddhists call a hungry ghost, a tortured character with a small mouth and huge belly who can never be satisfied. A representation of the unfillable void in all of us.

The funny thing, though, is that now that I can't run from what I perceived as ordinary, the ordinary is becoming more extraordinary. All the things I was intent on turning away from – the repetitiveness of the everyday, endless daily chores, seeing friends regularly: real life, in other words – are becoming beautiful to me. The simpler and more subtle life becomes, the more 'normal' things are becoming anything but, purely because I'm paying attention to them.

We don't have to go anywhere at all to experience life with a sense of adventure and openness. It all just depends on our state of mind and the way we perceive things. Which means that anywhere can become a portal to unimaginable adventures.

I'm finally understanding the truth behind Pico Iyer's words, from his 2014 book *The Art of Stillness*. 'In an age of speed ... nothing could be more invigorating than going slow. In an age of distraction, nothing can feel more luxurious than paying attention. And in an age of constant movement, nothing is more urgent than sitting still.'

Nowhere does this become more apparent to me than out in the bush. Every month or so now, when life begins to feel oppressive, Pete and I do what we now know works best to recalibrate our rattled minds and bodies. We throw the tent in the car and go bush.

Camping is both ethically and economically appealing. Although I've started teaching and running workshops and writing stories about sustainable travel, there has definitely been less money coming into our household and things have been very tight. Camping, happily, costs next to nothing.

Today, a Friday, is one of those days when we feel ourselves pawing the walls for an escape hatch. It's afternoon when we head a few hours inland to one of our favourite campgrounds. Even though the shadows are lengthening as we arrive, I head out for a bushwalk.

I have always been a walker. Dad's a cyclist, Mum's a walker: it's in my blood to move. I have walked my way back to myself all around the world. I've hiked through the Caucasus Mountains in Georgia, up a volcano in Papua New Guinea, and through minus 25 degrees in snowshoes in northern Japan. I walk to get myself clear, to find rhythm in my days, to get fresh air into my body and to clear out all the cobwebs. I walk and I walk. Eventually, I fall into a space that is quiet and calm, where there is nothing but my body and the world around it.

Today is no different. Walking through the bush, the spinning thoughts start to drift from my mind, leaving space for the living, breathing world to enter. The longer my hiking boots crunch along the trail, the more space there is, and the more I start to notice: fungi blooming from the scorched trunk of a eucalypt, the lazy drone of pollen-drunk bees hovering over frothy white wildflowers, the flurried swish of a lizard taking cover under a nearby wattle bush. By the time I arrive back at camp, I feel altogether more human, altogether more part of the interconnected web of life surrounding me.

By now, Pete has made a roaring fire and is starting to cook dinner over the campfire griddle. 'How good is this?' he yells. I don't even have to reply because I know he knows I know. I get to work putting up our tent. I know this makes me a bit of a freak, but this is one of my favourite parts of the camping experience. I love the focus it demands. I roll out the plastic groundsheet and the rough canvas over the top, hammer in the steel pegs, prop up the central pole. Then I fill our newly created home with our thin, narrow camping mattresses and sleeping bags and pillows. Putting up a tent reminds me of setting up cubby houses as a kid and the feeling of safety, but also of freedom, it always brought to create a little world of my own.

As I work, my mind drifts back to an assignment I took in Mongolia years ago, where almost half the population still live as nomads. I spent three days with a nomadic family out in the endless steppe, living in a *ger* tent, surrounded by nothing but grassland and yaks and wild horses. I helped the family erect their round *ger* and set all of their worldly possessions up inside it. Together, we milked their mares to make cheese and cream, and I watched them slaughter a goat and use every last piece for food and clothing. At night, I sat with them around a bonfire taller than my head, drinking too much yak vodka, singing folk songs and learning to play the 'finger game', the addictive Mongolian version of rock paper scissors.

There was such a feeling of tranquillity pervading the lives of the Mongolian nomads, such a sense of enoughness. Maybe they were so content because they'd never had more and had nothing to compare their lives with. Or maybe they weren't as content as I perceived them to be. I don't know. But I remember how I felt being around them – calm and centred and whole. In my life I have wanted, desperately, to hold on to those feelings, but they have regularly slipped out of my grasp. The prickling feeling that there is never enough time and always something more and better to do has been ever-present in my life until recently. Even when I was doing 'relaxing' things, they were scheduled, to make sure they fitted into days that were always bulging at the seams. A typical daily schedule of mine could look like this:

5am – meditate

5.20am – journal

5.40am – run

6.30am – breakfast, dress, read news, check email

8am – write story

12pm – lunch

12.30pm – write next story

3pm – odd jobs, clean house

3.30pm – write

5.30pm – prepare and eat dinner

6pm – bath

And on it went. No time for spontaneity. No time to just flop and look at the birds in the trees. Or if there was, it was in the schedule: twenty minutes for sitting and watching birds in trees. Anytime Pete would catch a glimpse of one of my lists, he would say there was no way a single human could get it all comfortably done in a week, let alone a single day. Where was the space for just enjoying life? he asked. Where was the ten-minute slot for 'give Pete a blow job'? It wasn't there. That's another reason why I loved travel writing (though it's not very cool to admit it): there were always hectic schedules, packed to the brim with too many activities that made me feel like I was seeing and doing as much as was humanly possible in any given day. It was exhausting. It still is exhausting. Camping, however, doesn't require schedules. In the bush, I can let go.

The fire beckons. Invites us for dinner. We throw a blanket out over the bare earth and join it, watching orange flames lick the blue night. Afterwards, we lie in our tent and peer out through the flaps as the sky shakes its stars at us. Enoughness fills me, rare as a blood moon, pushing the churning thoughts out of my ears until there is nothing, nothing, nothing left but complete presence. Nothing to be added to the moment to make it any better than it is right now.

At home I'm usually a very neurotic sleeper. I need an eye mask, silicone ear plugs, the bedroom to be as black as the dark side of the moon, socks, fresh air but not too much, a book and a glass of water by the bed, a doona that's just the right weight, and for Pete to stay on his side of the bed or, often, to not be in the bed at all so his symphonic snoring doesn't keep me up. Out here in the bush, though, it's enough to just roll over, let Pete become the big spoon, and let the croak and hum of the land send me to sleep.

~

It's 7am, and Pete and I are heading out to hike across Australia's largest granite rock formation. A 247-million-year-old chunk of stone towering 200 metres above the border between New South Wales and Queensland. The longer we walk, with thousands of hectares of bushland rolling out from all sides, the more I melt into the landscape around me. I breathe in and imagine the molecules of the eucalypts entering my body, seeping into the fractures in my nervous system and tranquillising my neural pathways. It's like a giant natural beta blocker.

As sunshine oozes over my bare shoulders, I imagine how the granite beneath my feet might have been carved by water, wind and ice over millions of years, and I am humbled. My footsteps become little invocations of gratitude: thank you, thank you, thank you.

This rush of ecological tenderness that often washes over me when

I'm hiking has a name. I know this because Mum texted it to me a month ago. I'm close to Mum and share most things with her, including my anxieties about our collective future and my desire to do better for the environment. She has similar concerns and never tells me I'm being over-the-top or alarmist, which makes me love her more. The word she sent me was soliphilia. Coined just over a decade ago by the Australian professor Glenn Albrecht, soliphilia expresses our love of the interconnectedness between each living thing, its ancestors and the environment it evolved in. Isn't that beautiful? It also includes our willingness to accept the responsibility to protect and conserve nature at all costs, and is the antidote to solastalgia, another term created by Albrecht to explain the deep sadness we feel witnessing the destruction of our planet.

I'm starting to feel soliphilia for this land I was born on, and it's because I've been forced to just be here. For the first time I have stayed, when all I've wanted to do is run.

When I'm out in the bush, I feel expanded, warm and bright. Like a cage full of rosellas has been opened inside my chest and they are all released and fluttering around in there. I feel my whole body opening and softening, just the way it does when I'm falling in love. Which is, I suppose, exactly what's happening out here. I think of all the people around the world who are feeling this sense of reconnection to the land they are stranded on right now. Who are finding a sense of stillness, and finding themselves and a sense of home inside that stillness. It makes me want to zip open my chest and watch those birds spread their wings wide and fly up into the sky.

9

Silence

Meditating towards myself

The first time I heard about Vipassana was about twelve years ago, while I was staying at a yoga ashram in Kerala, in south India. I met a German couple who'd just finished a ten-day Vipassana silent meditation retreat, and they were evangelical about it. They said it was the hardest thing they'd ever done, physically and mentally, but that it had rewired their brains and given them a new lease on life.

At the time, the idea terrified me. I told myself I could never do it. I had meditated on and off for years, ever since a friend invited me to a meditation class when we were eighteen because 'the monk was so hot'. Vipassana, though, sounded like a form of torture. I once heard Tim Ferriss talking on a podcast about one he'd done and about how it had unearthed abuse he'd suffered as a child. He didn't sleep while on the retreat, he said, and it made him feel as though he was having a psychotic breakdown.

For someone whose brain is as skittish as mine, Ferriss's story sounded alarm bells. Aside from the obsessive list-making and the extreme sleep sensitivity, there are other neuroses I contend with on a daily basis. I obsessively count my steps on my phone in the Health app, and if I don't get to the recommended 10,000 every day, I have been known to dance in the living room or pace around the house until I get there. If I can't make it to 10,000, I add more steps onto the following day to make up for it. When I go for long walks, I barely ever just walk – I will also talk on the phone, listen to a podcast or music, send messages, answer emails, take photos for Instagram or add to my ever-lengthening to-do list. Sometimes I do all of these things on a single walk. I always know what time it is, and how much time I have to do the thing I'm currently doing, because it never feels as though there is enough of it. What I'm trying to say is that I was convinced I'd emerge from a hundred-plus hours of meditation in a straitjacket.

But Vipassana kept showing up in my life, the way a friend you've fallen out with keeps showing up at events you've been invited to, reminding you of your unfinished business. Every few months I'd hear of or meet someone else who'd done a Vipassana retreat and whose life had changed because of it. I read an interview with the *Sapiens* author Yuval Noah Harari, in which he described Vipassana as the most important learning experience of his life and attributed his brightest ideas to it. Each time I discovered another detail like this, it felt less like a coincidence and more like a kind of calling.

To be clear, I have tried almost every form of healing and self-discovery technique I have come across. Most of the spiritual seeking started when

Pete and I lived in India. That year I had several appointments with a twelfth-generation shadow reader on a scorching Mumbai rooftop, who measured my shadow and read inscriptions on ancient palm leaves and told me I was born in India in a previous lifetime. I had my astrological chart read in a Varanasi back alley and went on a two-week tarot tour of South India. I travelled to Rishikesh to visit the ashram where the Beatles found enlightenment, and to Kerala to stay in a yoga ashram opposite a lion sanctuary. I whirled and chanted and meditated an illness into existence at the Osho ashram in Pune and was cursed by an angry eunuch in Delhi. I even applied my own urine to my face after a shaman told me it would heal my acne in Pondicherry.

All this spiritual questing didn't give me any solid answers, but it did addle me completely. Which, at the time, was exactly what I was after. To be opened up, to be muddled by unanswerable questions, to be confronted by the mystical, the strange, the unsettling, the chaotic. All the things my safe, stable upbringing was not.

After that year in India, the questing continued, a lot of it through work. I covered Buddhist retreats in Vietnam and Nepal, yoga ashrams in India, rounding retreats in Bali. They were all powerful and beautiful, but most of them just seemed to scrape the surface. The magic dust they left on me always seemed to drift away after a few days or weeks. When I told people this, the reply was often, 'But have you tried Vipassana?' There came a point when I could no longer ignore it.

After almost two years without overseas travel, the next time the craving for an escape hatch arises, I book myself into the nearest Australian

Vipassana retreat. As it's mid-winter, I pack a small bag with one pair of jeans, one pair of trousers, two jumpers, some woollen thermals, a beanie, a puffer jacket, a rubber hot water bottle, two thick pairs of socks and some Teva sandals, and off I go to become a monk for ten days. It will be ten days of nothing but silence, meditating from 4.30am to 9pm, with short breaks for meals and rest.

I am petrified.

~

Here I am. Suitcase in hand, waving goodbye to Pete as he pulls out of the car park with my contraband wallet and mobile phone, already asking myself, *What the hell have you done?*

I ask myself this question many times during my first night at the centre. I ask it when I'm making up my bed – a single plastic-covered mattress in a bunk room with five strangers and no heater, despite it being about 4 degrees after dark. I ask it when we're told, during the evening briefing, that for the next ten days dinner will be two pieces of fruit and a cup of tea. I definitely ask it when I sit for the first one-hour meditation and feel every muscle and bone in my body screaming with pain.

In Sanskrit, the word *vipassana* means 'to see things as they really are'. Rather than distracting yourself or papering over anything with mantras or visualisations, the Vipassana instruction is simple: focus on your breath and bodily sensations. Through witnessing these, practitioners believe, you can train yourself to stop reacting to the hardships of life. Change is inherent in all existence, says the Vipassana philosophy, so we may as well release control and accept things as they are.

Vipassana was the meditation technique the Buddha was using when he became enlightened under the Bodhi tree in India in 500 BC. This heartens me. It was handed down from teacher to teacher until it finally landed with the late SN Goenka, an Indian who was born and raised in Myanmar, where he learned the Vipassana technique from monks. Goenka's courses are now taught in about 140 centres around the world. It's his soporific voice that rings out into the meditation hall the first time we meditate, giving instructions to focus solely on our breath. It's his round, smiling face that appears on a large screen at the end of the day to give a 'dharma talk' about Buddhist philosophy, to help us make sense of the torture.

~

The first three days, we focus entirely on the sensation of our breath falling on the triangular patch below our nose and above our upper lip. Which sounds easy, until you consider doing it for almost thirteen hours straight, three days in a row.

We're instructed not to try to make the breath deep or long or 'meditative', but to simply focus on it as it is. A clear analogy for the acceptance of life in general. When unwanted things happen in life, most of us create a whole drama around it and make ourselves miserable in the process. This misery then projects onto everyone we come into contact with. Vipassana, we're told, will help us come out of this.

On day one, however, focusing on anything at all for more than two seconds is impossible. I wake at 4am and head into the meditation hall with about forty of the eighty other meditators (about half meditate in their rooms for this first session), and thoughts immediately start crashing through my mind. The thoughts aren't distinct and there is no logical sequence to them. There are fragments of thoughts, snippets of memories, and my mind flickers over hundreds of them a minute, like one of those old-timey film projectors. My mind whirls like a spinning top, oscillating between memories of the past and projections of the future. It does not want to stay in the present moment. The noise of these thoughts thrashing about in my head is terrifying, and by about 6am I'm realising an alarming truth: my brain is slightly broken.

It is physically very painful, too. Burning sensations zigzag through my body in waves, pains I have never experienced before. I often have a sore neck, but here it's my back that hurts. My right leg goes to sleep, then my left leg. I adjust myself: roll my shoulders, massage my back, take some deep breaths. I try a round meditation cushion, straddling it like a horse, then change to a meditation stool. That becomes uncomfortable, so I stack a couple of pillows on top of it. Soon that feels too high, so I try the cushion again, and the whole process starts over.

In the short breaks between sessions, which are presided over by a short-haired Buddhist nun who sits silently up the front observing each meditation session, we shuffle like 95-year-olds between our rooms and the dining room and the meditation hall – heads down, eyes on our feet.

There's to be no communication in here, not even glances or gestures, and I realise how much joy smiling or saying 'hi' to strangers usually brings me.

'This is actually a deep surgical operation of your own mind,' says Goenka on the video at the end of day one. 'When you open a wound, pus comes to the surface – it is unpleasant, but you have to accept it to fix the wound.' The same is true of our minds. The excessive, crashing thoughts are the pus that needs to be extracted. This will be uncomfortable, and we will want to run away, but we must make a 'strong determination', as Goenka puts it. His point is that we can only change the behaviour patterns of our minds by facing them, and I get it. But doing that is torture and I want nothing more than to flee.

Solace comes, however, in the form of the garden. This Vipassana centre is set on a hillside surrounded by bushland and faces a forested mountain. I can hear a rushing stream at the bottom of the hill, but a rope marking the centre's boundaries cuts us off a few metres before that. What's inside this rope, our territory, is a rolling lawn with half-a-dozen tall trees at the top and a semicircle of boulders towards the bottom. During the breaks I, like a handful of others, stroll around the edge of the lawn, or sprawl out beneath the trees to stretch my back and rest. Because, who knew, sitting in one spot and breathing all day long is one of the most exhausting things you can do.

We're instructed not to meditate outside, because the light and the breeze will be too distracting. After all that time inside, the fresh air and sunlight feel especially delicious against my skin.

~

In the evening dharma talk on day two, Goenka describes the mind as a wild bull. 'But a wise person trains this wild bull,' he says in his lilting voice, 'working patiently and persistently, turning its strength into service.'

This is important. Because no one can harm us more than our own wild mind, but no one can help us more than our own trained mind. By focusing on my breath, by day three I notice that while my mind is still kicking and bucking, gaps start opening up between my thoughts. The gaps are not even a second long, but they give me a disproportionate amount of hope.

Something else I notice, during these first painful few days, are the stories I tell myself about everyone else in the course. Students who've finished Vipassana courses before sit in the first two rows, and there's one woman with curly dark hair I can't take my eyes off. My mind latches on to her, like a leech on to an exposed ankle. I decide she thinks she's superior to everyone else, and find her to be supremely annoying, but also think perhaps I should be more like her. I watch her as she walks slowly and deliberately along the pathways, scowling and never lifting her eyes off the ground. I tell myself I too must walk more slowly and stop making eye contact with and smiling at everyone. I watch her as she eats, gazing lovingly at her food for minutes before she starts eating. I feel like throwing my fork at her. But I also remember a Buddhist meditation retreat I once covered in Vietnam where the monks said that by looking at your food before eating it, you can recognise all the elements – the rain, sunshine and air, and the work of the farmers and chefs – that have come together to make your meal. *Maybe she fancies herself a monk,* I sneer internally. I watch her as she sits for meditation, expertly adjusting blankets and pillows around her before sitting ramrod straight and not moving for the full hour.

Everything I see makes me think: *I hate that curly-haired woman.* And: *I must be more like that curly-haired woman.*

She is the picture of grace and nonchalance. So when she disappears in the middle of day three, I am completely thrown. *Surely she couldn't have left. Could she have left? If she can't make it, what hope is there for any of us? Who will I direct my scorn at now? How could she have abandoned us? How could she have abandoned* me? My mind loops on the curly-haired woman's absence for days after she leaves.

As horrific as it all is, though, I am determined to stick it out, no matter what. I feel sure that if we want to right our wonky world, we're going to have to fundamentally change who we are and the cultural priorities, desires and aversions of our entire society. I suspect one way we can do that is by breaking apart our own brains and putting them back together again.

~

Just when I've got the hang of focusing on my breath, the entire program changes on day four. Goenka's recorded voice instructs us to start scanning

129

down our bodies, starting at the top of the head. We must focus on each individual body part – eyes, nose, ears, cheeks, neck, shoulders – down, down, down, waiting to feel a sensation on each before reaching the toes and starting again from the head. Over and over again.

The sensation could be anything. It could be a pain, cold or heat, tingling or numbness, it doesn't matter. What matters is that we don't react to what we find. This practice is about realising that every sensation will eventually pass, and that everything in the entire universe is constantly changing. '*Anicca, anicca, anicca*,' says Goenka over and over again, using the Pali word for 'impermanence' to reiterate the Buddhist doctrine.

I find these whole-body scans easier, in one way, because they give my brain more to focus on and space to move around. I also find them harder, because it's almost impossible to stay focused until I reach my toes, and I constantly have to begin all over again as Goenka says we must when our attention drifts. But by starting to accept physical pains as unavoidable (there's a burning sensation in my lower back that's particularly niggly) and noticing how they eventually dissolve and disintegrate when I focus on them, I begin to understand I can do the same thing with emotional pain.

This all becomes clearer during the 'hours of strong determination'. These three one-hour sessions, during which we're not allowed to move our bodies *at all* for the entire sixty minutes, begin from day four. No more changing my sitting posture, scratching my face, adjusting my hair, stretching or any of the other things I've been doing to subtly distract and soothe myself. These hours feel endless, and I keep thinking someone must have forgotten to signal the end of the session. *Sweet Jesus, somebody help me.*

It's at about this time that I start thinking obsessively about sex. My mind clings to past sexual encounters and fantasies that play on an endless loop in my mind, like a porn clip you can't get off your desktop. I sit and I sit, and as I repeat the body scans, I feel my face and groin flushing with heat.

On day one, we committed to five precepts while on the retreat. No killing, no stealing, no lying, no intoxicants, no sexual misconduct. This last one includes masturbation. But after twenty-four hours of thinking almost solely about sex I can no longer bear it. I rush to the communal bathroom during one of the breaks, lock the cubicle door, unbutton my jeans, and masturbate furiously up against the door. I come quickly, my whole body seeming to explode into my hand, and I'm immediately regretful and full of shame. I feel like a gigantic failure.

Back in the meditation hall, I imagine the teacher can smell sex on me, can see the flush in my cheeks. That everyone in the hall can smell it and see it on me. The embarrassment and shame blooms up through my body in a warm wave. But the longer I sit with that sensation, the more I understand that this self-flagellation is supremely unhelpful. What has happened has happened. Goenka has this phrase, 'as the seed is, so the fruit shall be'. If I'm constantly planting seeds of negativity inside by beating myself up, nothing good will grow from me. So I make a pact with myself, there and then. I will be kinder to myself.

If there's one certainty in life it's that I, like all of us, will continue to screw up. Every day, in small ways, and every so often in much larger ways too. Dwelling on those mistakes, though, will help no one. *I will choose love*, I promise myself, because you can only give out the love you give to yourself. And if there's one thing the world needs now, it's what Burt Bacharach said it needed back in 1965 – love, sweet love.

~

Everything starts to change at around this point. It's like someone has pushed the slow-motion button on life. I become a sloth, focusing on each foot as it presses onto the earth, and on every mouthful of food I eat. I become a little like the curly-haired woman, actually.

The meditations are still mostly tedious. Once a day, we must now also sit in front of the Buddhist nun teacher for five minutes while she watches us meditate, and yesterday while she was observing me, I was stifling the need to cough so intensely that tears started oozing out of my closed eyes. When I opened them, the nun smiled at me, thinking, I suppose, that I was in such a state of bliss that I had started to cry. I smiled back, thinking, *Lady, you have no idea*.

I still have to keep reminding my brain to return to now when it runs off to replay scenes from the past or the future. But the point is that it does return, again and again. And if it's true that the only cure for distraction is attention, and that happiness can really only be found in the present moment, then that return is quite something.

When I scan my body, I start to feel what Goenka has been talking about, which until now seemed like total nonsense. I feel the vibrations, or wavelets, or subatomic particles running through me, through all of us, through every living thing – the very essence of life that connects us all. As strange as it sounds, I feel like a living, breathing Van Gogh painting: a mass of millions of wiggling brush strokes.

Life also becomes sharper, clearer. It's like a magnifying glass has been placed over my view of the world, and it becomes achingly beautiful. One afternoon, I walk out onto the lawn between meditations, and see another woman I've been feeling an intense *aversion* to, as Goenka would word it. She has been wearing this ridiculous furry brown bear hat the whole time, and hugging trees in the breaks. I watch as she drops to the ground and buries her face ecstatically in the grass, and instead of wanting to punch her as I have every other day, I think, *Yes, that's it!* That's what we need to do. Just love it all, and each other, as fiercely as we can. Because this life is singular and precious, and we're all just masses of vibrating atoms trying to fight our way through the confusion and be loved.

On the second-last night, I do what I've been doing every night at 'dinner' and take my fruit and tea and hot water bottle out onto the lawn. I lie there, wrapped in my puffer jacket and beanie, looking up at the night. As I look at the outline of the mountain etched against the sky and the scrap of new moon above it, I watch the earth and the moon pull away from each other. *I am watching the world turn,* I think, realising it's the first time in my life I have witnessed that. This miraculous thing that's happening every moment of every day, that I've never sat still long enough to watch.

I arrived here filled with fear that I'd go mad from endless hours of meditation. But the real madness is the speed I scramble around at, and my resistance to sitting and facing life, just as it is.

I'm realising that most of us cram so many things into each day to give the illusion that we're on top of things, that we're barely aware of what we're doing most of the time. But none of the supposedly urgent things we hurtle through our days attending to could be more urgent than this: slowing down enough to actually enjoy our lives – our utterly majestic, magnificent lives – rather than sleepwalking through them.

~

There is a wonderful story Goenka tells on one of the final days. It's about an Indian mother who sends her son with an empty bottle to buy oil from the nearby grocer. The boy goes and has the bottle filled, but as he's returning, he falls and spills half, and returns to his mother crying, 'Oh, I lost half the oil!'

The mother then sends her second son to do the same job. He also has the bottle filled, but is also clumsy and falls and spills half on his way home. This boy, however, returns very happily, saying to his mother, 'The bottle could have broken, but I saved half of the oil!'

The mother, a little exasperated now and still dissatisfied with the amount of oil she has, sends her third son. He also, you guessed it, falls and drops the bottle, spilling half. Like the second son, he returns to

Changing the way we travel can lead to a more abundant, healthy future for all life on earth and protect the very species we travel to see – like this mother and baby polar bear in the Canadian Arctic.

Overlooking the otherworldly rock formations in Warrumbungle National Park in New South Wales. We protect what we love, so by surrounding ourselves with nature during our travels we'll be more likely to fight for it when we return home. *Photo credit: Peter Windrim*

Volunteering at a regenerative 'syntropic' farm in the Northern Rivers region of New South Wales. Learning to restore the ecosystem while feeding the community through this kind of farming can help us bring the planet back into balance.

Feeling 'soliphilia' – a rush of ecological tenderness – while hiking across Australia's largest granite rock formation at the border between New South Wales and Queensland. Through soliphilia we express our love of the interconnectedness between each living thing, its ancestors and the environment it evolved in.

Weaving around the sedimentary sandstone cliffs of Western Australia's Kimberley coast – one of the world's last true wildernesses – on a Zodiac, while learning how to become better environmental stewards of the land.

Soaking up the phytoncides, the natural oils inside trees that are part of their defence and communication systems, helps us feel calm and clear. *Photo credit: Peter Windrim*

Rabari tribesmen usher their herd of goats off the road in the Godwar region of Rajasthan in India, where the degradation of farmland has forced goatherds into urban areas. We pass them as we make our way to a conservation-focused camp that's bringing life back to a formerly degraded area of farmland.

Visiting the artisans of Saheli Women, who make ethical clothes and revive handicrafts in Rajasthan. Saheli's travel offering allows visitors to learn about and help preserve important Indian artisanal techniques.

A Rajasthani elder plays the tabla drum during a small ceremony inside the Saheli Women's temple. In a world where we're acutely aware of fashion's environmental offences and human-rights violations, it feels important to spend time with the makers of the clothes we all wear.

The sacred confluence of the Bhāgīrathī and Alaknanda rivers infuses the Indian town of Devprayag with a potent spiritual energy. It's the perfect place for contemplation and deep rest, which allows us to get in touch with our biggest, boldest creative ideas that just might help save the world.

Flying over terraced farmland on the way to Phaplu in the Nepalese Himalayas, gaining a deeper understanding of the fabric of the land and of my place in the order of things.

The Happy House, a traditional stacked-stone Sherpa house in Phaplu, is a base for explorers and creatives wanting to take part in impactful regenerative travel. Where you choose to stay is a big part of travelling ethically, and the Happy House reinvests its profits into local social projects such as funding the hospital and monastery.

Nepalese prayer flags adorn a bridge on the way to Thupten Chöling monastery. These flags are believed to absorb compassion and goodwill and radiate it out into the world, and act as a call to awareness for mindful travellers.

Following a Sherpa guide through the Magic Forest. Sherpa people, who originally migrated to Nepal from Tibet five hundred years ago, regard Solukhumbu as a beyul, or sacred valley.

Blessings at 9,000 feet, arriving at Chiwong Monastery in Nepal's remote Solukhumbu district. It was tempting to stay with the monks but, for now at least, I must be out in the world. There is work to be done.
Photo credit: Alexandra Lewis

We all need our climate totems. Some people have whales or koalas; I now have this psychedelic rainbow comb jelly. *Photo credit: Daniel Stricker*

his mother very happy, 'Mother, I saved half the oil!' But this boy is a Vipassana boy. Full not only of optimism, but also of realism, he says to his mother, 'Now I'll go to the market, work hard the whole day, earn five rupees, and get the other half of the bottle filled.'

This, says Goenka, is the Vipassana mindset. Optimistic, but also realistic, and with a strong work ethic at its core.

Of the many deep and profound lessons these ten days have taught me, I predict this will be the one that stays with me longest. The planet we love has changed, and is continuing to change, that much is clear. Falling into a puddle of despair over that, however, isn't going to solve anything. The earth doesn't need our tears and our sadness, our heavy hearts and our endless sighs. It needs our love and our optimism. These things will help us keep our heads above water when the tempests come, and help us stay present and alive to all that's still left to be saved. And it's only from a place of love that we'll be able to do the good, hard work that's needed to set things back on the right track.

~

When Pete picks me up on day eleven, I am tender and teary, brimming over with love and gratitude. This has been, without a doubt, one of the most difficult experiences of my life. I am proud of myself for sticking it out. Now that I've done this one hard thing, I know I'll be better equipped to deal with other hard things in life. And I'm praying that everything I've learned doesn't slip from my fingers, like that bottle of oil in the three clumsy sons' hands, as soon as I'm no longer sequestered from the corrupting influence of society.

We walk through the car park, the morning light bouncing off tree leaves shivering in the winter breeze, and I say a teary goodbye to two guys climbing into their van. 'Did you make friends with those guys?' asks Pete. I say no, I don't even recall seeing them in there, I just love and feel very connected to everybody and everything right now. He nods, unable to hide a look of bemusement, and I wonder if he thinks I've lost the plot. Maybe I have.

We start driving home, but within five minutes we're brought to a halt at some roadworks on a hilltop, by a guy in a high-vis vest holding a stop sign. Pete winds down his window and the guy strolls over and leans his elbows on the window ledge. 'Sorry, guys, should only be a coupla minutes,' he drawls, fixing us with his clear blue eyes and gesturing to the excavator inching its way across the road. 'But, gawd, isn't this a beaut mornin'?'

He starts talking about how he quit his soul-crushing corporate job a few years ago, and how grateful he is that this job lets him be outside all day. 'I mean, look at this view, would ya?' he says, sweeping his arm out across the valley. An awestruck, inspired road worker? Well, I never. It all feels very *Truman Show*-esque, and I start to wonder if it could be possible that the Vipassana centre *planted* this guy here. But no. This is merely the universe working in its mysterious ways. We drive away, and I am speechless. Humbled by this reminder that wonder and magic really are all around us, all of the time, if only we open our eyes wide enough to see it.

10

Water

Rising together in the floods

It's a question we've all considered at least once in our lives. If your house was on fire and you could grab only a few things, what would they be? I always answered, with great certainty, that it would be photographs, my passport and my laptop. Maybe a few of my favourite pieces of jewellery. Only it turns out that today, a day when I've had to make that very decision, I'm taking nothing of the sort.

Our house isn't burning, but floodwaters in our region are rapidly rising after days of ceaseless rain, and we've received a text from emergency services saying we need to evacuate. It's Monday morning, and an hour ago Pete and I were in bed, arguing about something, talking about the week ahead, listening to the rain drum on the roof. It wasn't until we turned our phones on and lots of text messages pinged through from family and friends asking if we were okay that we realised something was terribly wrong.

We jumped out of bed and hurried, bleary-eyed, to our front deck to see a foot of water rising quickly over the front garden. Our suburb doesn't have paved roads or gutters, so we've seen water pool before, but never anything like this.

Now that we're alerted, we start madly googling and calling around to friends, trying to get our heads around what's happening. An unprecedented amount of rain is falling on our region. The nearby town of Lismore is already underwater, and Mum is sending texts saying if the levee there breaks, the situation here could change very quickly. The water has already risen too high above the road leading out of our suburb, so we can't drive. We need to get out. And we need to get Milka out. She's 40 kilos and we can't carry her, so we have to leave while the waters are still shallow enough for her to wade through.

Pete runs outside to move our two cars to higher ground. There's a cafe at the end of our street that long-term locals say the water has never reached before. That's where Pete's headed. Meanwhile, I grab a small olive-green backpack and start filling it. Not with our favourite travel treasures – the wooden stool we bought in Ethiopia, or the beaten silver peacock from India – and not even the framed photograph of Pete's mum. I take practical things. Our favourite alpaca blanket, our toothbrushes, spare undies and a few clothes. Our mobile phones.

Everything else precious we stack up off the floor. Our laptops go up on the top shelf in the kitchen, the TV goes on the couch. I'm busy rolling our expensive woollen rug up when the power goes out. Ten minutes later, Pete is back and says we have to go.

Outside, the water isn't surging in a gigantic wave like I'd always imagined it would in a flood, but rising quickly and steadily. It's already halfway up our thighs. There are people on kayaks and dinghies paddling around the streets, and the eerie sound of an emergency chopper fills the air. We slip along the muddy bush path beside the river, the water already lapping at the elevated banks, cross the wooden footbridge and walk up two more streets. Finally, we reach the local church, which has opened as a temporary evacuation centre. A fitting location for a weather event of such biblical proportions.

The afternoon starts to blur at this point. More people and kids and dogs arrive, and Milka starts snarling with agitation. The apple-cheeked Fijian pastor makes everyone cups of instant Nescafé and sits in the corner singing and strumming songs on his acoustic guitar. The phone lines go down, and we decide that our close friends and neighbours, who thought the waters wouldn't rise as quickly as they have and decided to stay home with their babies, have to evacuate. Pete heads back out into the lashing rain and the rising floodwaters to get them. He goes, and I start to spiral, imagining all of them being swept off down the river. Before too long, though, they turn up, including our friend Em, in her undies and bra, with her baby on her shoulders. We all cry with relief and fear and love.

By now, the centre is crammed with about fifty people and Milka is losing it, barking and nipping at little kids and other dogs. It's all too much, but we can't leave because we don't have a car. Our friends say they have their two four-wheel drives with them, and we can take one, but we have to go now because the water is rising and the highway is about to close. Then suddenly we're in the car and driving, we have no idea to where – just anywhere away from the water. We end up in the hinterland town where we used to live, driving aimlessly until we find ourselves at our English friend Hannah's house. She's opening the door and we're hugging and I'm crying and she's saying stay as long as you like, Mummy is here. Then suddenly her mum, Robyn, really is there, pulling my body into hers with her strong arms and telling me she's drawn a bath and would-I-like-some-tea and don't-worry-everything-will-be-okay.

I just cry and cry and wonder whether our house has been washed away yet.

~

I'm lying in the bath at Hannah's, the steam curling into the autumn air. My body, stiff with exhaustion and stress, is slowly unwinding. That is until a friend calls, speaking at 100 miles an hour and telling me that fuel is running out, money is running out, the apocalypse is here, and we'd better be prepared. The world suddenly seems unstable again, and I yo-yo like this the whole night, depending on who I speak to.

When Robyn feeds us handmade pasta and red wine and listens to our worst fears, I feel safe. When one of our best friends, who lives in the hills next to a river, calls us on a crackling phone line and tells us she and her two kids, both under ten, can no longer leave, I feel terrified. When Pete wraps me in his arms in bed and tells me everything will be all right as long as we have each other, I think maybe he's right and I feel calm.

For most of my adult life, I have had the sense that home was not where I lived, but what lived inside me, or something along those lines. Now that I'm imagining our house filling with water and the possessions we've accumulated over a lifetime floating down the street, though, I realise my physical home *does* matter to me. A lot. It doesn't matter because of the things inside it; the evacuation process and how little we took with us made that very clear. It matters because it's where our memories are stored, and where our memories are made with family and friends and community. It matters because it's where we feel, or *felt*, safe. It matters because it's the place I go to recalibrate when the world becomes too much, and I need to hide from everything and find myself again. I've always fancied myself a nomad, but this experience is making me realise how precious the notion of home really is.

~

Twenty-four hours later, the rain eases and it's time to head home to see if our house is still standing. On the drive back, the scenes on the street are apocalyptic. There are lines of cars snaking down the street waiting for fuel, because of circulating rumours that no more fuel will be arriving for weeks. Supermarket shelves are half empty because everyone's panic buying, and there are hour-long waits at the few cash machines that actually have cash in them.

We make our way to our suburb, parking on the other side of the river because the road into ours is still flooded. My hands shake as we cross the bridge, passing a friend's house that's half a metre under water, then turn to walk along the muddy river path. When we reach our cul-de-sac, we have to wade back into waist-high floodwater covered in rubbish and a slick of grime and oil from all the dead cars. It's as if we're entering an alternate reality, where the usual order of the world has been shifted slightly. With each step the rushing of blood in my ears becomes louder and louder, as does my prayer – to whom, I'm not quite sure, but there it is: *Please let our home be okay, please let our home be okay, please please please please please let our home be okay.*

And then, there it is. Our front garden covered in chest-high water, our veggie beds and outdoor bath and Pete's surfboards floating around the side of the house like sinking dinghies, the small timber office we built in our backyard filled with half a metre of water. When we wade up the front steps of our home, though, we find that by some miracle, the flood-waters have stopped two centimetres below the floorboards. We walk in the front door and my knees buckle, then I'm on the floor on my hands and knees, kissing the floor and sobbing and saying, 'Thank you, thank you, thank you,' over and over again.

Our two cars, however, weren't so lucky. Both of them have been written off. I didn't own a car until I was thirty-four and splashed out on my ten-year-old BMW convertible, Cindy, when I finally bought one. It was the most impractical car I could think of, one that would entice me into driving by making it more fun than I naturally found it. I called her Cindy because she reminded me of a Barbie car, and Cindy became the fulcrum of so many fun-filled days and nights out with our friends. She even had her own playlist called *Pop That Top*, featuring Cyndi Lauper and Whitney Houston. Her glovebox was filled with lollipops and the headscarves that I'd urge my friends to put on anytime I put the top down.

I loved that when we drove Cindy with the top down, I was immersed in the world through all my senses. I loved that I could be open to the breeze, that I could smell the wildflowers and the fields after the rain, that when Pete was driving I could lie back and watch the light winking through the trees or gaze up in wonder at blinking stars. I loved that Cindy embodied the parts of myself – the carefree, silly, sparkly ones – that I sometimes found it hard to express in other ways. I've been threatening to trade her in for something more practical for months. Now that the floodwaters have taken her away before I was really ready, though, I am unexpectedly sad.

~

The waterlogged single mattress needs four of us to pick it up and heft it out the open window. It hits the metre of water covering the street below with a gigantic splash. We wipe our muddy gloved hands on our shorts, and turn back to survey the mud-slicked house we're in, looking for what needs to be chucked next. A breeze blows through the window, bringing with it the rank stink of sewage, and I have to breathe deeply through my mouth to stop myself from throwing up.

We've spent the past two days here in the small coastal town of Woodburn, one of the worst affected areas, as part of the 'mud army' –

thousands of volunteers who are helping clear out flooded homes all up and down the coast. Rather than sending in troops and personnel to help with this extraordinary destruction, our government has kept them on 'standby'. In response, we've set our anger and frustration aside and turned to each other, dropping everything to try to mitigate the devastation.

We've been mucking toxic sewage-laden mud out of strangers' homes and scrubbing those homes with squeegees and gurneys and toothbrushes in the hopes they might become liveable again. We've been handing out food and water and fresh towels and cleaning supplies and vitamins, and we've been hauling people's mud- and sewage-soaked belongings onto the footpath – people who had little and now have far less. We do this before going home to cry and do our paid jobs and try to put our own flood-impacted houses back together again.

Today we're helping a guy named Jason, who has four kids and another on the way. He put every dollar he had into his two-bedroom fibro house, passed down to him from his mum. This morning, Jason pointed out his mother's ashes, sitting in a little wooden box on a sodden shelf, while we threw all his worldly possessions out the window and tried to save what we could. He asked us to try to save his television, even though it had been submerged for twelve days. His sodden curtains too, and the hinges and handles on the cupboards in his small kitchen. 'They're expensive, those things, y'know,' he said as his eyes filled with tears.

Of course, Jason can't afford flood insurance, which can cost up to $25,000 a year in areas vulnerable to floods. Of course, he will continue living in a house that will now likely be mouldy and unsafe and unhealthy for him and his kids. What other choice does he have? It's people like Jason who are hit hardest by the climate crisis, I think, as I continue gathering his sodden books and kids' toys and cans of baked beans and soup that might have been contaminated by the toxic sewage and petrol-laced waters and toss them out the window into the enormous rubbish pile.

~

Someone has made a hand-painted psychedelic sign and propped it up out the front of our local community hall that reads, 'Not all heroes wear capes'. That has been the overarching message during the first few days of this catastrophe. It has been astonishing watching everyone rise up and help in their own ways. Together, we've become our own mycelial network, feeding and loving and supporting each other. Together, we've become a single heroic being who has continued to rise, day after exhausting day, with a cape woven of determination and ferocity and courage.

As devastating as they've been, the floods have brought out the gifts in us all. They have been a potent reminder that we are what we give, not what we have, and that true wealth means having enough to share. We've had friends deploying helicopters and heading out on death-defying rescue missions in dinghies and jet skis and kayaks. Friends with babies, frustrated about not being able to leave home, are tirelessly washing and cooking for both victims and helpers, while others still are organising fundraising, shelter and care.

One of our friends bought everyone in our group veggie boxes and delivered them to our houses, knowing fresh food was hard to come by. Another friend bought jerry cans of fuel and risked their life driving up into the hills, surrounded by landslides, to deliver them to houses that had been cut off. We've had strangers in our own home, too, a team of four who turned up at our door with gurneys and cleaning products, offering to muck out our flooded office and help us put the garden back together.

The thing is that none of us, including me, know what we're doing. When Pete and I arrived at Jason's waterlogged, mud-slathered house, there was a moment of hesitation before we walked through the door. Was it too invasive? Was there someone better equipped than us to help? Were we going to be safe in there? But then we cast all those doubts aside and simply did what needed to be done, knowing our togetherness is all we have.

~

On the way home from Jason's, we drive through suburb after suburb with streets lined with piles of sodden mattresses and cupboards and couches and chairs and toys and clothes and dishwashers and fridges piled higher than the houses they're in front of. I cry at the terrible waste of it all.

At home, I take a shower and scrub the thick, stinking mud off my body. The water supply was turned off for days, and now that it's back on it seems like an unfathomable luxury. I boil some water and steep a cup of tea. Then I plonk down on the couch next to the TV that we still haven't had time to put back in its usual spot and reflect on this past surreal week. I reflect on the devastating losses and the eye-watering frustrations, the hard fact that this flood is yet another consequence of the resource-heavy lifestyles of those of us in the Global North, and on the tiny and huge acts of kindness that have pulled us all through.

As our planet continues to warm, and these disasters strike increasingly often, this kind of community uprising and resilience is what we'll need. I look out the window at our garden, slowly drying up in the sun, and think about how the world would change if we could harness this community spirit all the time. I imagine what our days might look like if collaboration took precedence over competition and what possibilities might arise if we chose to consistently support and heal each other, while healing the land around us.

In a trembling world, our most powerful choices are to remember we are so much more capable than we think we are. To recognise that thriving is only possible if we nurture strong bonds with our communities. And, as the waters of life rise, to simply reach out our hands and help each other.

~

It's Saturday night and hundreds of our community are crammed into the local pub by the beach, dancing like wild things as the rain pours down outside. Since the flood a few weeks ago, dozens of recovery fundraisers have been organised in our shire. This one has seen our kind-of-famous DJ friend bring the more famous DJ Floating Points

147

to town. The cavernous room is throbbing with deep house, and Pete and I and our best friends – the ones who almost lost their house in the hills – are on the fringe of the crowd of steaming bodies, sweat-lathered, arms raised, dancing away the pain and exhaustion and sadness and loss of the past month.

When Floating Points starts playing a remix of The Pointer Sisters' disco classic 'I'll Get By Without You', we all go nuts. We reach our hands out across the sea of bodies to each other as lightning cracks overhead, laughing and singing and hugging and dancing, dancing, dancing. Skirts hitched, boots stomping, eyes closed, hearts open. It is a moment of pure elevation, a collective scream of 'WE MADE IT' shouted through hundreds of dancing bodies. It is a disappearance into a moment of dizzy, voluptuous joy, in the midst of one of the worst moments of our lives.

It's only when the song has finished and the lights have come on and our DJ friend is hugging me that I see that he – this cool guy in sweat pants and a tie-dyed tee who lost his own home to the flood – has tears of pain and relief and joy dripping down his face. The French philosopher André Gide once called joy 'a moral obligation'. Joy is necessary even in – or perhaps *especially* in – our darkest days, because it is the very thing that lifts us up out of the muck, liberates our spirits, and helps push us through another precious day on earth.

As Pete and I walk out hand in hand into the wet dark night, I swear I can almost see the joy: a sparkle, a puff of phosphorescence, glowing around our bodies and lifting our spirits up towards the sky.

11

Tree

Forest bathing in the Southern Highlands

Sit by some water, the stream, a waterfall. Spend time sharing your dreams with the water. Know that sometime in the future, the dreams you send into the water will come back to you.

I'm deep in a lush gully in the Southern Highlands, resisting the urge to roll my eyes at the prompt I've just been handed. For the past three days, I've been led through a handful of activities – 'invitations', as our guide, Christie Little, calls them – just like this, as part of a 'forest bathing' retreat I'm on with seven other women. Each of us has been handed a different instruction scribbled on a folded white card, all designed to help us connect to water. We're to seek out our own spaces in the bush in which to ponder them.

I walk for a few minutes until I'm alone, then sit on a warm rock and put my card down beside me. I wonder if Christie realises how ironic this prompt is for me. My relationship to water has changed since last

149

month's floods. It has been carrying dreams away lately, not bringing them towards me. Many of our friends are still homeless and will be for months to come, the relief efforts are still continuing, and we're all ragged and wondering what this means for the future of our region. What used to seem calming and purifying now seems dangerous and potentially life-threatening. Fear has crept silently in through the back door and chased trust out, and I want it to return.

And so, I close my eyes and ask the water to help me learn to trust it again. To help me find a way back to a world where we're all trying harder to be a beneficial presence for the natural world and its waters. I put my hand in the stream and let the clear water rush around it, cooling my blood, cooling my bones, cooling my mind. It sounds nice, but what does it really mean to be a beneficial presence for the water? I start to think of all the ways I haven't been that in my life. Images of the synthetically dyed clothes in my wardrobe bubble up in my mind, the run-off from which seeps into and poisons our water systems. I also think about the chemical products I've wiped onto my body and the bleach I've put on my hair that runs back into the water system, and of the water I've wasted on long showers and baths. Looking into the stream, I promise the water I'll try harder to do less of the things that harm it. That I will think about it when I bathe in it, swim in it, and drink it in. That I will be grateful for it.

~

The tiny grasshopper carefully steps her way across the leaf, adjusting her long antennae, as the light rain sifts down around her like icing sugar on a cake. She lifts a cantilevered hind leg and shakes off a water droplet, then rolls onto her torso to dry her left side. Her enormous black eyes take in the world around her, including me, the giant with the staring eyes as big as her own body. I'm transfixed by her delicate ballet, my attention zooming so far in that all the mental chatter stops and I'm simply *here*.

Which means, I guess, that this retreat is delivering on its promise. 'Immerse yourself in the forest, absorb its sights, sounds, and smells, and you will reap numerous psychological and physiological benefits,' read their website invitation. After the nerve-crunching devastation of the floods, I suspected it would be the perfect medicine.

Our guide for these three days is the aforementioned Christie, a petite blonde holistic psychotherapist and counsellor, and the first person in New South Wales to become an internationally accredited 'nature and forest therapy guide'. As she explained last night over dinner at the historic house we're staying in, forest bathing is essentially a mindful, sensory experience in nature. It isn't focused on the body, as a regular bushwalk might be, and it's not focused on the mind either, as with other nature walks where you learn the names and characteristics of plants. Forest bathing is about slowly connecting to and contemplating a landscape, through a series of guided exercises focused on attention, in a way that's said to hugely benefit our tech-addled brains and fried modern nervous systems.

'Nature is the therapist, I'm just the guide showing the way,' says

Christie – who, after working as a burnout coach for big multinational companies, eventually burned out herself. Around that time, she learned about this thing called forest bathing, which reduced the biomarkers of stress, improved the functioning of the immune system and enhanced mood, creativity and attention span. She immediately decided it was something she needed to pursue and to teach, since she knew firsthand that she was far from the only one burning out.

On this cold, grey morning out in the manicured country-style gardens surrounding the house, Christie leads us through something called 'pleasures of presence'. Standing in a small circle under a pagoda, she invites us to first close our eyes and focus on what we can hear and smell and feel around us, then walk as slowly as we can through the gardens. Keeping every movement as slow and intentional as possible is key, so we can really notice what we notice in each moment, using all our senses. As Christie says, 'Anxiety lives in the past or the future, it's very rarely in the present moment, so the gateway to that is through the senses.'

I walk through the light rain, pressing my feet slowly and deliberately onto the earth, and stop to burrow my nose deep into a lavender bush. The floral scent climbs up into my nostrils and spreads up towards my brain, diffusing through my nervous system. I crouch down to stroke the fuzzy leaves of a lamb's ear plant and draw crisp winter air laced with sap and fresh cut grass deep into my lungs.

They're simple acts of connection, things I would have done as a kid, when I had hours on end to just play in our garden and climb the jacaranda and get to know every plant and flower and insect. I'm surprised how centred and *good* they make me feel.

Feeling good is really what forest bathing has been focused on, ever since the term was coined in Japan, where it's called *shinrin-yoku*, in 1982. The Forest Agency of Japan started promoting the mental and physical benefits of being present in the forest in 1982 because, horrifyingly, the rates of *karoshi*, or 'sudden death by overwork', were on the up. Hundreds of people in Japan were dying each year from heart attacks and strokes brought on by work stress.

These nature-connection techniques, of course, aren't new. Indigenous communities around the world, including the traditional custodians of the land we're standing on right now, the Gundungurra people, have been connecting to the natural world in this way since time immemorial. It wasn't a 'technique' Indigenous communities had to learn, but a practice and a way of being in and relating to the world that was embedded and passed down intergenerationally.

It's a connection that has clearly been lost in recent decades, as we spend far more time with our noses buried in our devices than we do outside. Our lives have become so full of convenience and comfort that we've mostly stopped relying on and paying attention to nature. Considering the rising number of catastrophic weather events due to the climate crisis, the disconnect is as harmful for the natural world as it is for ourselves.

The next invitation from Christie is to find an analogy for ourselves in the garden, something in the natural world that mirrors how we feel internally. I walk for a few minutes before stopping in front of a white agapanthus with a vine curling up its tall stalk, the light green leaves reaching up towards the bulbous head of white flowers. In that simple conjoining of plant species, there's a beautiful support system on display. Without the agapanthus, there'd be no way for the vine to reach the light. It makes me think of our community during the floods – how we all needed each other's support to get through the trauma and find our way back to the light. And how we are all interconnected and entwined, so that without each other, we might very well wither and die.

Nature, of course, is full of metaphor. When we come back together to share what we've discovered, there are stories of resilience and vulnerability, loss and joy, beauty and pain, all being mirrored by this small patch of earth. Christie talks about a bush she saw with no foliage, how it made her think of the space she was in three years ago when her husband died unexpectedly. She talks about how she has used the remedial power of nature to slowly return from that dark place. Nature really is the great healer. Finally, we are remembering that.

~

Given the combination of fresh air, physical activity and no technology, it's no surprise that most of us also say we feel more relaxed and focused after the session. Christie says this is also thanks to phytoncides, the natural oils inside trees that are part of their defence and communication systems, which also boost our immune systems.

Research backs this up. A 2010 study by Tokyo's Nippon Medical

School, for example, took groups to forest bathe in twenty-four forests across Japan and found they had lower levels of the stress hormone cortisol, lower blood pressure and lower heart rates, when compared to the other groups who were taken for a walk through a city. Studies from other countries, including Finland and the US, showed similar reductions in anxiety and stress.

A 2009 study from South Korea put three groups suffering from major depressive disorders through four therapy sessions in three different environments: a forest, a hospital and regular psychotherapy. The forest group saw a remission rate three times higher than those in hospital, and twelve times higher than outpatient psychotherapy.

In tandem with suggesting nature might be one of our most potent medicines, these studies hint at something Christie describes as 'small ego, large self', which happens when we're in nature. 'Being in a flourishing natural environment reminds us that we matter less than we think we do,' she says as we drive into a nearby national park for the afternoon, 'and that can be a really good thing for our mental and physical health.'

This ego diminishment is one of the first things I notice when Christie asks us to find a 'sit spot', which she describes as 'a place you choose to sit, in observation and reverence to the environment'. It's usually a place you'd return to each day, observing the subtle changes in the environment over time, through different seasons and weather events. Christie tells us to find a 'sit spot' a few minutes' walk from where we're standing, and to write, draw or simply sit and observe what we see around us.

By now the sun is shining, and I follow a narrow path about 50 metres down into a gully, past glistening grass trees and whispering she-oaks, and stop in front of a sheer, moss-covered rock face. I sit on a fallen log, moisture quickly seeping through my jeans, and watch water droplets dripping from spongy pillows of moss. I notice different kinds of moss, some like mini staghorns, others like tiny tree ferns. The wet velveteen surface seems to ask me to touch it, so I do; to sniff it, and when I do I think of sauerkraut; to open my mouth and inhale the wet air.

The longer I sit, the more the rock face reveals to me: the little ants rushing over it, so busy and full of purpose; the way the filtered light is sifting through the canopy and playing across the moss, creating abstract, fractal patterns; the sound the wind makes as it moves through the trees, a shushing that reminds me to think less and listen more.

There's a word the Japanese have for feelings that are too deep for words. *Yūgen* is that which gives us a profound sense of the mystery and beauty of the universe. The more time I sit and stare at the mossy rock face, the more I feel myself fall into that mystery. The biggest mistake we may have made as humans is to get so busy we don't have any time left just to sit and be with nature. This is where we lived for most of our life on earth. It's only recently that we've become so divorced from it. No wonder so many of us feel lost and unaccountably sad. We have, essentially, rendered ourselves homeless.

Soon, after what feels like a few minutes but could very well have been an hour, Christie calls us back and introduces us to another technique. 'In Japan, they call this "meeting a tree". I invite you to take a slow walk and choose a tree, then just be with it for a while. You might talk to it; some people breathe with it or even sing to it – whatever feels good to you.'

I walk back out into the bush, far enough so that I leave everyone behind. I keep going until I see a magnificent ancient eucalypt that reaches its soaring branches down to me and demands that I stand with it. Its trunk is scorched from the bushfires, and it's so wide my arms would have to be four times as long as they are to reach all the way around it. I look up at the tree and something starts to happen that I know will forever change the progression of my life. Almost like when I first met Pete when I was the mature-age work experience girl at the media company he worked at and when we were introduced to each other our eyes locked, and his sparked in a certain way, and we both smiled and laughed and knew, instantly, that everything had changed, even though we hadn't yet spoken more than five words to each other, and I went home that night and told Mum I'd met the man I was going to marry. Something like that.

What happens is that I start to talk to the tree. And the tree starts to talk to me.

I look up into the canopy and place the palms of my hands on the rough, charred trunk. I just stand there like that for a moment, breathing and watching and waiting. I think about the energy pulsing through the tree, and the energy pulsing through me, and how every single living thing on earth shares this very energy. The mushrooms and the Vipassana and our garden and our community showed me the pathway to this feeling of universal oneness, but now it is ingrained in me, and I can access it whenever I want.

I feel a sudden urge to ask the tree something. In my mind I say something like, 'Hello, beautiful eucalypt, I love you. I know you've suffered, I've suffered too, and I'd like to do something for you. Can you tell me what you need?' Then I stand there and wait, for what I'm not exactly sure, I just know I need to stay calm and still. But then everything in my head goes kind of silent and I hear a voice. Not the tree's voice exactly, but my own voice, emanating from deep inside. From that primal, ancient place that knows all things and is deeply connected to all things.

The voice says, *Just be with me.*

I wait for more, cock my head and crane my neck and listen for it, but there is no more. Just that simple phrase, repeated over and over in my head like a mantra.

Just be with me.

Just be with me.

Just be with me.

And that, I suppose, is as simple as it needs to be. Because it's what we all know, deep inside. That the right way to live is in a way that puts nature at the centre of things. That is where we belong, where we feel most centred and restored and calm. Where we feel most ourselves.

Also, on a more basic level, if we're spending more time in nature, we're likely spending less time doing the things that are burning holes in our souls, and in the atmosphere. Things like wandering around shopping malls like zombies, buying things we mostly don't need or even probably want if we thought harder about it. Things like hurtling around town in our gas-guzzling cars, between all the meet-ups and commitments we've said yes to even though we probably don't even want to go. Things like buzzing around the planet in planes too often, burning massive amounts of fossil fuel, because we haven't stood still for long enough to see how our actions are harming the very planet we're travelling to see.

Soon, I hear a 'cooee' reverberate through the forest, pulling me out of my reverie. I run my palms over the tree's trunk in thanks, and as I do I notice a split in the rough-charred bark and push two of my fingers inside, feeling the soft, smooth layer of new bark sitting just beneath. It is the perfect farewell from my new friend: a small but mighty reminder of the unstoppable, regenerative power of nature that gives me a surge of hopefulness about the future of our planet. Maybe, I think, as I slowly walk back to the group, if we all spend a little more intentional, immersive time in nature, we can learn to be a more regenerative force for nature right back.

~

Back home in the months that follow, we slowly bring our garden back to life, and I find my own sit spot. I return to it day after day, to tune in to the daily and seasonal changes around me, and to myself.

When we bought this house, we decided to do something that seemed extravagant and plumb in an outdoor bath, which I'd dreamt of doing for as long as I can remember. Pete bought me the vintage mint-green bathtub from an antiques warehouse when we lived in the Hunter Valley, and it has travelled with us to two houses since. Back in the Hunter, it sat in our garden without plumbing and we'd fill it with endless pots and kettles of boiling water until it was full and we could lie under the black sky and stargaze until it went cold. That was until we realised we could dig a hole under it, fill it with wood, and make a roaring fire that would almost boil the water. We had to put a wooden bathmat into the steaming water, to sit on so we didn't burn our bits while we bathed, but otherwise it was as close to perfect as you can imagine.

Now, though, the small bathtub has hot water plumbed directly into it. Every few days I fill it half-full, sink my body into the warm water, and soak and look and listen.

I remember Sylvia Plath writing in *The Bell Jar*, 'There must be quite a few things a hot bath won't cure, but I don't know many of them. Whenever I'm sad I'm going to die, or so nervous I can't sleep, or in love with somebody I won't be seeing for a week, I slump down just so far and then I say: "I'll go take a hot bath."'

Yep, I thought when I first read it, *a bath's the cure for everything*. But put that bath outside, out in the wind and the sunshine and the rain, out where flowers and leaves and soil and salty air can drift into it, out where you can hear the birds singing and the trees sighing and the insects humming, and it's taken to a whole new level.

Over the past two months, since we got the tub back into place after the floods and cleaned it out and started using it again, it has become my sit spot. When I go out there, I try not to bring my phone or book or anything with me. I just soak and look and listen.

There are two gigantic, ancient eucalypts at the bottom of the garden, twice as tall as our house and as old as time itself. When I lie back in the bath, my view is of them. I'm learning the patterns of our little piece of land from this old tub. If I bathe at dusk, I watch the brush turkeys heave their bulbous brown bodies up and up through the boughs to their roosting positions, and I listen to the kookaburras send their goodnight-world laughter out into the gloaming. If I bathe at dawn, I watch those same treetops come alive with magpies and rainbow lorikeets and other small birds I don't yet know the names of, all gathering and gossiping and prepping for the day ahead. I've drunk tea and burned incense and journalled in this tub. Just last week, one of my oldest friends came over and we drank wine and ate pizza in here together, talking and laughing until night-time came and our fingers and toes became prunes and the water went cold.

This morning as I lie in here, watching the winter sun glance off the water and cast abstract patterns against the wooden fence, and listening to the distant sea crash and the occasional shriek of the neighbours' kids, I notice how all the plants we've nurtured over the past year, most of which were hardly affected by the flood, are coming along. The saltbush by the side of the house isn't growing as well as the kangaroo paws, and it might need to be moved. The pandanus palm's spiny leaves seem to be the spider's favourite web scaffolding. The billy buttons, with their fuzzy blond heads, are dying, and I make a mental note to find out why.

This bath is the place where I connect most intimately with our garden. Here, I edge a bit closer to ancestral ways of bathing, when we always cleaned our bodies outside in natural waterways. And if I sit here for long enough, I forget myself entirely and become water, earth, wind, trees and sky.

12

Mother

Connecting in the Kimberley

Leaning back in our inflatable Zodiac, Mum and I watch hundreds of seabirds – cormorants and frigatebirds, terns and curlews, boobies and noddies – wheel across the sharp blue sky. I take Mum's delicate hand, smaller now than it used to be, and give it a squeeze. She was nervous about taking this trip, a seven-day expedition cruise along Western Australia's Kimberley coast, her first trip since before Covid. But as we watch the birds' gentle ballet and listen to their caws, I know Mum's feeling the same as me: if we had wings, we'd be soaring too.

I'm a little ashamed to admit it, but in ten years of travel writing, this is the first assignment I've taken Mum on. There's been lots of talk over the years of her joining various trips, but in the end it always seemed too difficult or the timing was off or my itinerary was too packed.

In the early months of Covid, though, Mum had a heart attack. She didn't need a bypass or a stent or anything, but it did land her in hospital in the middle of lockdowns, which meant neither my older sister nor I could visit. It came as a shock since she's one of the healthiest humans I know. She carefully watches what she eats and walks every day, sometimes for five hours at a time, and she could easily pass for a decade younger than her seventy-one years.

Mum's heart attack was a timely reminder: none of us knows how long we've got on this earth, so putting things off is a fool's game. I promised myself then that I wouldn't miss one more opportunity to celebrate the woman who gave me life. When the Kimberley assignment came up, I pushed Mum to come, doing what I could to assuage her nervousness about travelling with a heart condition during a pandemic. As our Zodiac circles Adele Island, one of 2500 islands scattered along this coastline, with thousands of seabirds floating above and around us like confetti, I'm so happy she took the risk.

It feels right to be exploring this natural wonderland with Mum. She's not the most adventurous human – you'd have to pay her to go camping or on a multi-day hiking trip. But she loves the natural world and taught me to always take care of our ultimate mother, the Earth. Since I was a kid, I've watched her do things like wash out plastic rubbish bags so she can reuse the same one for months on end, put buckets in our shower to collect the wasted water for the garden, and hold on to pieces of clothing for decades because she doesn't want them to end up in landfill.

When I once asked her as a child if we could please, pleeeease get juice poppers when we were doing the weekly food shop at Woolworths, she pulled a pack off the shelf and began explaining. 'You see this plastic?'

she asked me, pointing to the lining holding the six small juice boxes together. 'You see the plastic straws on each popper, and the plastic those straws are wrapped in? Where do you think that's all going to go, once you've drunk the juice? So you see why we don't buy poppers,' she said, putting them back on the supermarket shelf.

I felt embarrassed by a lot of this at the time. I felt embarrassed when I pulled my recycled Peter's ice-cream container lunchbox from my backpack and had to explain to the other kids why my sandwich was wrapped in paper instead of plastic. Or by the fact that some of my clothes were hand-me-downs. Now, though, I love Mum for giving a damn and for inadvertently teaching me that environmental stewardship doesn't have to look just one way. You don't necessarily have to have your hands in the dirt every day, or be out protesting every weekend, or go hiking or camping all the time. You just have to love the earth and take that love into account when you're doing everyday things in your life.

We learn by observing our elders. By watching Mum take care of Earth this way, I have become an environmental steward, too. I've always wanted to make her proud, and I still do. Doing right by the strong, discerning woman who brought me into this world is one of the driving forces of my life.

~

'This is one of the world's last true wildernesses,' says our guide, a young marine biologist named Kieran with a five o'clock shadow and a sparkle in his eye, the next afternoon as we putter along canals lined with thick mangroves in a place called Talbot Bay. 'A lot of it is either national park or managed by Indigenous communities, so it's 98 per cent untouched.'

It certainly looks untouched as we weave around craggy sedimentary sandstone cliffs that look like ancient, ruined cities, painted deep oranges, greys and whites from leaching minerals. Around 1.8 billion years ago, says Kieran, the Kimberley was a separate land mass that collided with the ancient Pilbara and Yilgarn regions. This formed the core of the Australian continent, a fact that Mum and I agree leaves us feeling as though we're standing on the edge of time itself.

Kieran points to the mountains towering around us and interlaces his fingers to explain how they are the remnants of the collision. The crumpled layers of these mountains tell us about the shaping of Australia, he says, and how it has been carved over billions of years by wind and water. We sit in silence, letting the timelessness of this land settle into our bones and feeling far less important than we did a few minutes ago. The heat in the Kimberley ripples and throbs, weighing on our bodies and whispering to us to slow down. It feels good to just sit and listen to the emerald water slap against the side of the Zodiac for a while.

With a roar of the engine, we're dashing off again towards *Garaanngaddim*, the Horizontal Waterfalls, which David Attenborough called one of the greatest natural wonders of the world. We round a corner and, suddenly, there are the falls, rushing through a narrow gap in the soaring, rust-red McLarty Range, like water being sucked down a plughole. The Kimberley is famous for its enormous tides, and here the

10-metre tidal fall pulls up to one million litres a second through the gap. Imagine a waterfall that has fallen onto its side, and that's what you have here.

'Ready?' asks Kieran. I turn to check in with Mum, who's usually nervous about these sorts of things, but her hazel eyes are flashing with excitement. We grab hold of a rope strung across the centre of the boat to keep us steady and zoom towards the waterfall at high speed, our Zodiac dancing wildly over eddies and whirlpools, and then we are, incredibly, bumping along the waterfall itself, feeling like we're riding a bucking bull. We shriek as the spray spangles us and our butts hit the rubber side of the Zodiac, and I hear Mum's laughter ring out over the rushing of the falls.

I look over at Mum – at her face that is my face, with its proud nose, deep-set eyes and wild dyed-blonde hair – and think about how coming into a deeper relationship with the land I was born on means coming into a deeper relationship with the woman I was born from.

It's so easy for us to criticise our mothers. We can blame them for everything we perceive as wrong with ourselves and our lives. I did that for a long time, blaming Mum for not outwardly displaying as much physical affection as I would have liked or expressing her love with words – both reflections of her own upbringing – or for pushing me hard as a kid so that I learned to push myself hard and as a result became very anxious in my late teens. But I reached a point a couple of years ago when I understood that holding on to that criticism and resentment serves nobody, and that it was blurring my ability to see all the sacrifices she and my dad had made for us and all the ways they *were* expressing their love. I realised that for everything I thought Mum did 'wrong' at the time, there were two other things she did right. That her 'love language' is acts of service rather than words, and that's okay. And that I wouldn't be the hardworking, risk-taking woman I am today if it weren't for both her encouragements and restrictions.

I look around at the turquoise waters and burnished cliffs and these words bubble up in my mind.

I am her.

She is me.

We're both these rocks.

We're both this sea.

~

We cruise further up the coast overnight, the slurp of the sea against the side of the ship lulling me and Mum to sleep in our little wood-panelled cabin, with its two single beds set side by side. Late the next morning, we're out on Zodiacs again, darting across the sea in search of Australia's own Atlantis.

The Kimberley's 400-square-kilometre Montgomery Reef rises up and out of the ocean each day as the tide goes out, a phenomenon that's unique in the world. Its existence relies on enormous tides, like the 4- to 10-metre tides here, and on being composed of the type of reef that can survive coming in and out of the water twice a day.

Within minutes, our Zodiac slips into the main channel that snakes through the exposed coral reef. We watch in disbelief as it emerges from the sea like some gigantic ancient tortoise, with hundreds of mini cascades pouring off the top. Egrets and frigatebirds fall from the sky like blowing sparks to grab their morning seafood feast from the small sinkholes pock-marking the reef. A green sea turtle scuttles back to the safety of the sea, joining dozens more turtles popping their gleaming heads up all around us.

Our guide points to a few small globs of land on the eastern edge of the reef, known as the High Cliffy Islands, and tells us they were once home to a tribe that mysteriously disappeared. 'The Yawijibaya lived on the main island, which is only one kilometre long and three hundred metres wide, for almost seven thousand years,' he says, shielding his eyes from the late-morning sun as it winks off the reef.

The lives of the Yawijibaya, a tribe of about three hundred that were nicknamed the 'giants of the north' since some were said to stand seven feet tall, were intertwined with the massive tides. They'd ride the currents out to Montgomery Reef on mangrove rafts to collect sea turtles and dugongs, stingrays and fish to eat. In 1929, a film crew videoed the Yawijibaya fishing and rafting and carrying 150-kilogram sea turtles across their shoulders, but when they returned soon after to do more research, the tribe had vanished without a trace. 'There are stories of tsunamis and tribal wars, even about alien abductions,' says our guide. 'But the most sensible and likely theory is they just integrated into other Aboriginal communities around the area.'

Whether the cause was supernatural or something more prosaic, the disappearance of the Yawijibaya remains one of Australia's greatest mysteries, and only enhances how intriguing Montgomery Reef really is. While coral reefs around the world are facing an uncertain future because of rising ocean temperatures, Montgomery has become remarkably robust. This reef can handle temperature and environment change, because it happens every day when it comes out of the water. Our guide tells us that scientists are actually taking coral from this reef and planting it on the Great Barrier Reef, to see whether it will be able to withstand the rising temperatures there.

I catch Mum's eye and smile. I know she worries about the world her grandchildren – my sister's three kids – are inheriting, and about the kind of future they'll have in a warming world. But this tale of Montgomery's resilience brings with it hope for the future of the planet, and, for me, a renewed desire to help conserve and steward it.

~

Later, after a sun-splashed lunch on the back deck of the ship, Mum and I are lazing around our cabin. The afternoon is hot and bright, so we leave the balcony doors open and let the ocean breeze waft through the curtains. We're sprawled limply on our single beds, Mum looking through her photos from the day as I read my book. It's called *The Most Important Job in the World*, written by an Australian journalist named Gina Rushton, and it's centred around the question of whether or not we should become parents.

This question has skulked around the edges of my consciousness for years, trying to find a way into my busy mind, my busy life. It's a question that's linked to so many other questions, related to purpose and legacy and time. The book investigates a lot of them. Should we have children in an era of climate breakdown? How do you balance ascending careers with declining fertility? Does entering motherhood mean giving up your dreams?

For years, my travel writing career helped Pete and me push this question to the side. We aren't people who 'just know' whether we want to have children or not, and for a long time we were able to blame our hectic travel and work schedules on our indecision. We were busy living our fabulously unfettered dream lives and didn't really see how a small child fitted into a life spent snowshoeing in Japan and learning to weave in remote parts of Guatemala – or, in Pete's case, making wine and building bars and spending hours on end reading and gardening and cooking lavish meals.

Since the pandemic hit and all the travel and busyness came to a grinding halt, though, we still don't have a clear answer. We remain ambivalent. We vacillate between 'I don't feel compelled to have children' and 'What if I regret not having had children?' while the biological clock continues to tick. We are, we believe, one of those couples who could be perfectly happy without children, yet that doesn't necessarily mean we wouldn't also be perfectly happy with children.

It is confusing.

I've tried all kinds of healing and therapy and written endless lists and journal entries but, still, the answer isn't clear. I'm curious about how it would feel to care about another being more than myself – which, if I'm being honest, I haven't really felt yet. But Pete and I are both scared of giving up the life we've created together, and also mildly terrified of what we see around us: those strung-out, tired women who've given away such huge chunks of themselves in order to give to this other being that there's only a sliver left of the women we once knew. The complaining I hear about how little time and freedom my mum-friends have, about how strained their relationships are, about how they don't have time to read or think or do much of anything for themselves anymore adds to this terror.

I'm also scared of making a mistake. Of having a baby and then hating it, as the worst part of me worries I will, but not being able to reverse the irreversible. I'm doubtful, too, about whether, on an ailing planet, so much of our love should be funnelled into one other human being, or whether the best job for that love to do in the world would be to give it to the waterways and the forests, to the animals facing extinction and the insects that are predicted to all but disappear over the next decade, to all the existing humans who desperately need more love and resources and help.

Could mothering simply mean loving our dog, Milka? Could it mean loving our garden? Could it mean loving our friends and family and all of their kids? Could it mean loving writing and creating, and hoping that can be its own kind of mothering? Could it mean loving the world that spins around us, and every creature on it?

Another book I read recently – the heart-wrenchingly beautiful

Stranger Care: a memoir of loving what isn't ours by Sarah Sentilles – has also helped me navigate this space. Sentilles expresses ideas about love that have changed me and opened me in unexpected ways. She writes about this kind of 'other mothering':

'"Do you have kids?" strangers asked almost every day.

'"No," I said, not wanting to explain, because, really, it's an unimaginative question for anyone with a complicated relationship to family making, for those of us who've experienced miscarriage or failed adoptions or the death of a child, for those of us estranged or embattled or in grief. It's a question I now refuse to ask. "Tell me about your family," I say instead, because I know belonging comes in all shapes and sizes, visible and invisible, hidden and made and chosen and found.'

I look over at Mum and watch her flicking the edge of the blanket between her thumb and middle finger the way I've watched her do whenever she's deep in thought, ever since I was a kid. I think of the beautiful friendship that has formed between the two of us, and how I would want that sort of relationship with my child, too. I think of all the powerful lessons she has taught me, and about how I'd like to pass those lessons on to someone else one day.

At dusk, when Mum and I are drinking pina coladas together while watching the sun set the ancient rock formations on fire from the top deck, I think that maybe I need to stop thinking. Instead, I could let the love that floods my body when I'm with my mum, doing things like this, lead the way.

Maybe it's time to close my eyes and jump.

~

If our ship were to sink this morning, leaving us stranded in this cove that's accessible only by boat or helicopter, our only hope for survival would surely be Naomi Peters. Our young guide from the local Arraluli clan spends seven months a year in the Kimberley's remote Freshwater Cove, where Mum and I have found ourselves on our final morning. Naomi shares her intimate knowledge of Country with passing travellers through her family's company, Wijingarra Tours.

'We're trying to educate people on preserving what we have left,' says Naomi, gesturing to the land her ancestors have stewarded for tens of thousands of years. Naomi's mother Isobel started the Arraluli Whale Sanctuary Project, to protect the humpbacks that breed in Freshwater Cove each year, inspiring Naomi to spend the majority of her time back on Country.

Sharing oral stories passed down through the generations is an important element of Aboriginal culture, and a way of sharing lessons about caring for the earth. Before we head off for a bushwalk, Naomi shares one of the Dreamtime stories, ancient narratives that are woven throughout the traditional lands of the First Peoples. These stories carry knowledge about how the world was made, about the patterns that exist in the universe and about how to live in harmony with the natural world. The one Naomi tells is about two birds fighting over some bush honey, and how their subsequent bloodshed coloured the earth red.

'We get told this story when we're young so we learn to share,' says Naomi. 'A lot of our Dreamtime stories are very simple, but with important knowledge – knowledge people are only just realising the importance of now.'

As Naomi smears ochre paste on our cheeks to welcome us to her clan's land, I reflect on how we'll need this historic knowledge from the land's first caretakers to adapt to what's coming. For far too long, Australians have ignored the wisdom of First Nations people. The way we've treated our Aboriginal people is shameful and sad, and if we'd listened more to these people who knew the land – who have loved it and understood how to properly care for it for over 60,000 years – I'm convinced we wouldn't be in the situation we're in.

Soon, Naomi's brother Neil leads us on a hike through bushland dotted with cotton flowers, bottlebrush and wattle. Sweat trickles down my torso in cold rivulets as I duck beneath the branches of a Kakadu plum tree to get some refuge from the beating mid-morning sun.

We soon reach a rock chasm called Cyclone Cave, decorated with 4000-year-old rock art in the Wandjina style, which depicts ancestral beings that travelled through this region during the Dreamtime. Neil points out a stingray, the Arraluli clan's totem, and an impressive series of concentric circles that tell the story of a boy who went fishing without his mother's permission and drowned.

'Some of these are sad stories, but they're always about learning,' says Neil quietly. 'You've got to learn to listen, don't rush in life, wait your turn.'

The past two years have taught us all so much about exactly these things – learning to listen, to slow down, to be patient. These are truths Australia's First Nations peoples knew and lived by for millennia before settlers arrived on these shores. This is how they managed to successfully care for their environment for longer than any other group of human beings, until colonisation. If we'd championed First Nations voices and leadership from the start, instead of erasing, silencing and marginalising them, we wouldn't have had to learn these lessons in the painful way we have only started to over the past few years.

Soon, Mum and I hike back down to the cobalt sea, passing towering termite mounds and yellow coastal banksias along the way, to join Naomi down at the rock pools beside the shore. She tells us about the survey work she and her family are doing alongside scientists, including whale counts and new species discovery here at Freshwater Cove. She points out a freshwater spring bubbling up from the rocks, and as Mum and I crouch down to fill our aluminium bottles with water that tastes of sea and stone, she tells us why fewer and fewer young people are moving back onto Country. 'They like the ease of modern life, they can't do without phone or internet, they're used to the hustle and bustle,' she says. 'But me, I'm a very quiet person. I like it here.'

Looking out across this peaceful inlet, bombarded by wild rays of mid-morning sun, I can understand why. I hope that Naomi stays here and continues to pass on her wisdom. We need her knowledge, and the knowledge of indigenous peoples the world over, to protect the wild areas that remain.

To protect my mum's life. To protect my life. To protect all life on Earth.

13

Country

Listening to Tasmania's first stewards

I'm sitting by a roaring fire under a star-smattered sky in the Bay of Fires, on Tasmania's remote north-east coast, about to join a traditional Aboriginal smoking ceremony. It will cleanse me of any negative energies or spirits I might be carrying and open me up to Country, says one of our guides, Cody Gangell, a palawa man in his late twenties who's bent over the fire, stoking the flames.

Cody holds the delicate, narrow leaves of the black peppermint gum up to the firelight for my three travel companions – two other writers and a soft-featured woman named Gill, who manages the three-day Indigenous-owned wukalina Walk we're on – and me to see. It's the totem plant for his people, he says, connecting them to the spirits of their ancestors. The ancestors would be placed in the hollow of a peppermint gum tree and cremated there, so their remains would then nourish those trees and travel up into the leaves. By burning and breathing in these leaves, then, Cody is introducing his ancestors to us.

As I sit by the fire, I think about my own ancestors, who came to this country seventy years ago from Hungary, Poland and Russia to flee war in Europe. My ancestors were displaced and severed from their homeland and lost identities and homes and knowledge in the process, but they also found a new life and safe haven here. I think about how their stories must contribute to my sense of disconnection from Australia, and how their longing for their faraway homelands, where they'd felt a sense of belonging, would have also been passed down to me. I think about how little time I spend connecting with my ancestors, and how much richer my life might be if I did it more, reflecting on everything they might have to say to me and the guidance they might have to offer.

Be grateful to call this place home, Mum's Hungarian parents might say.

Don't turn your back on it, my Russian grandmother might say.

Cody places the peppermint gum leaves and the leaves of two more medicinal herbs, kunzea and tea tree, under the hot coals. When the smoke starts billowing, he shows us how to kneel down and scoop it over our faces and hair and down our necks and backs, while inhaling the medicinal oils of the plants. I drop to my knees and wash myself in smoke, closing my eyes and breathing in the vaporised plant oils, imagining the ancestor spirits welcoming me to this land.

Now that we have been properly introduced to the land, we settle back into our chairs. Cody shares two Dreamtime stories with us. With the crackle of the fire and the distant roar of the ocean as our soundtrack, the stories carry us out into the night.

~

The decision to come to Tasmania was an easy one. A few months ago, overseas travel opened up again for Australians, and invitations for foreign assignments started popping up in my inbox, like mushrooms on the lawn after heavy rain. I'm still feeling the urge to stay in Australia, though – still craving a deeper knowledge of, and intimacy with, the land on which I stand. I recently went to a talk by the renowned Aboriginal author Bruce Pascoe, who said, 'Like any relationship, if you spend time with country, you will be close again.' When I heard that, goosebumps spread across my forearms, the way they do whenever I hear something true and beautiful. The phrase has hovered in my mind ever since, reminding me of all the reasons why it's important for me to stay. When this opportunity came up to walk with Tasmanian Aboriginal people on their ancestral lands, to listen to their stories and participate in their cultural practices, which have been handed down for hundreds of generations, my entire body hummed *yessss*.

Before the smoking ceremony, we walked up to the top of the historic 1800s Eddystone Point lighthouse to look out over the iconic coastline. The tangerine-coloured granite boulders and the azure Tasman Sea stretching beyond them form the quintessential image of wild, untouched Tasmania. But as we watched the light drain from the day, Cody and Carleeta Thomas, another palawa guide in her early twenties, filled us in on the area's tragic history.

In palawa kani, *wukalina* – the Indigenous name for this part of

179

Tasmania – translates to 'woman's breast'. The palawa see this area as the nurturer of the whole of Australia, said Carleeta, spreading her arms wide to encompass the land and sea Country all around us. 'But wukalina is also very significant because it was from here that our mob would see the British ships arriving and light signal fires to let communities on the islands know they were coming,' she said. 'Basically, to hide the women and children.'

Carleeta then told us the harrowing history of the Black War, which officially began in 1824 but had begun brewing when the British first settled Tasmania in 1803. The brutality reached its peak in 1830 with a military offensive known as the Black Line, a human chain of colonists that moved south through the settled districts of Tasmania, intimidating, capturing, displacing and relocating the remaining Indigenous peoples. By then, Tasmania's Aboriginal population had dwindled to about two hundred, having been massacred, dispossessed and decimated by diseases. Any survivors of the Black Line were exiled to Wybalenna, a settlement on Flinders Island. Displaced, traumatised and plagued by disease and malnourishment, most died within a few years of arriving in the settlement, and by 1876 all but one of those who were considered the 'last remaining' Indigenous Tasmanians had passed away.

Carleeta's voice wavered with emotion as she told this traumatic colonial history: the dehumanisation, the loss of value and dignity, the decimation of her people's culture, and the loss of their land, ceremonies and languages. It made me sad that she had to relive it by telling it to travellers like us, especially since the ongoing effects are still felt by ancestral Tasmanians today. Less than 1 per cent of Tasmania's landmass has been returned as Aboriginal land, for one thing. The land we stood on is currently only on a forty-year lease to the palawa people. Later, though, as we sipped kunzea tea in the lounge room of the restored lighthouse keeper's cottage we were staying in, Cody explained that 'telling the story is one way of working towards understanding and reconciliation'.

His words are still echoing in my mind the next morning, as I pull on my beanie and gloves and take a steaming mug of tea out onto the back porch to watch the sun rise above the ocean, casting a luminous glow over the small brown wallabies feeding on the lawn. I listen to the murmur of the grasses and the eddies of the air, wondering whether we'll ever truly achieve reconciliation in this country after the atrocities that have happened. I think again about how painful that history must be to tell, about how painful it is even to hear. But it is the story of the making of this country. It is the story of the making of this world. This is what we humans do.

Turning away from this history because it's too painful to face isn't the answer. I know because that's what I've done for a long time, or at least, I haven't turned towards it. It just seemed too complex and too full of things I didn't understand. It was better, I told myself, if I just stayed away from it.

Instead of exploring the Indigenous culture of the country I was from, I chose instead to look at the indigenous cultures of faraway places. Learning about indigenous cultures in Ethiopia or Namibia or Peru seemed somehow less threatening, less uncomfortable. But travel isn't about staying comfortable. It's about opening us up and helping us learn, about breaking down barriers and collapsing false truths. And if we dismiss or turn away from our own uncomfortable colonial histories, we'll have little chance of avoiding the same mistakes in the future.

By staying quiet and listening to Cody and Carleeta share their stories, I'm starting to better understand how our country, how our world, got into the state it's in. This issue won't be an easy one to resolve, but simply shutting up and listening is a very good place to start.

I want to remember this as I walk this land over the next few days. I want to remember what a gift it is to walk and talk with smart, passionate palawa, to listen and ask questions and absorb some of their intimate knowledge of Country, and to share the time and space to understand the finer points of their complex history.

~

By 10am, Carleeta is driving me and one of the other journalists, a bubbly young woman with curly blonde hair named Elli, who reminds me of an adult version of Shirley Temple, through the bush in a four-wheel drive. The music's pumping, we're all talking and laughing, and I've just told Carleeta what a skilful driver she is when suddenly the car swerves on a muddy track and the back wheels start to spin. We're bogged.

Carleeta's mortified, promising this never, *ever* happens to her. Elli and I, however, are loving the unexpected turn of events. We jump out of the car to help, fossicking through the bush to try to find big logs to shove beneath the wheels. It's a lost cause: within minutes the car wheels are 30 centimetres deeper in the mud than they were before.

We're close to the start of today's hike, though, and I tell Carleeta we'll go find Cody and Gill and send them over to help. After a few minutes of walking, we find Gill waiting for us in her own four-wheel drive, but not Cody. He has already started the day's walk with James, the other writer, and Gill tells us to follow them while she goes to help Carleeta.

Elli and I start walking along the beach. The icy Antarctic winds are ripping across the sea and pushing us so hard it takes about seven steps to make it one metre forward. Powder-white sand flies into our faces, tears ooze down our cheeks, the turquoise ocean roars, and everything blows and moves and sparkles. I feel full of life and excitement and adventure.

We've been walking for almost an hour when we see two pairs of boots left at the bottom of some steep sand dunes. We look out over the luminous ocean, pull our puffer jackets closer around our bodies, and decide there's no way Cody and James would have gone swimming in the icy waters. Why on earth else would they have taken their boots off, though? We walk up into the dunes and laugh nervously as we joke that they've been abducted by serial killers. Just as we're about to give up and walk back down to the beach, a call gets carried towards us on the wind. Far off in the distance, we see two small barefoot figures walking along the sand.

Tromping closer to them in our hiking boots, we see one of them is waving their arms. It's Cody, running towards us yelling, 'Take your boots off!' He reaches us, out of breath, and tells us this is a huge midden, a kind of enormous open-air museum littered with tens of thousands of oyster shells and bones and small stone tools that were used by Cody's ancestors up to 12,000 years ago. We quickly pull off our boots and walk barefoot along the icy wet sand so as not to disturb anything, while terns and oystercatchers wheel overhead. Cody shows us how to identify which stones were tools, and what they might have been used for. When I marvel at the ingenuity of his ancestors, Cody shoots me a wry smile.

'We've been managing this land for forty-eight thousand years; we know a thing or two.'

We continue walking along the windswept beach, past shark eggs, dried sea sponges as delicate as French lace, abalone shells shining iridescent purples and greens in the sharp shards of winter sunlight, and bull kelp as thick as leather. Cody stops to gather up armfuls of the kelp and pulls little light brown berries off it, handing them to us to eat. They taste like popcorn, he says, and when we burst them between our teeth, we discover they do.

What Cody's ancestors also knew well was how to shelter in Tasmania's often harsh and unforgiving environment. We soon arrive at wukalina's *krakani lumi*, an architecturally designed camp that mimics the traditional seasonal bark huts of Tasmania's First Nations peoples. To get there, we follow a trail fringed by squat *yamina* grass trees thrusting out of the earth like green pompoms, and eucalypts with thick lips of fungi pouting from their trunks. There's a large open-fronted central room with a wood-panelled domed ceiling, and five small standalone sleeping huts scattered throughout the scrub-throttled bushland where, in the summer, we would have spent the night. Made of native timber that has been charred to protect against bushfires, the structures rest on footings that have no long-term impact on the site, and run on solar power, rainwater, and thermal heating and cooling. They are elegant and beautiful, and I wish I could stay here forever.

We spend the afternoon at the camp, where Carleeta and Cody teach us basket weaving, using the collected bull kelp, twine making from river reeds, and shell necklace stringing – the oldest continuing cultural practice in Tasmania, which is still handed down through the generations.

This is an important way of connecting to Elders, and of sharing stories, says Carleeta. We sit around the outdoor fire rolling river reed into twine, a process that's harder than it looks. It takes time and attention and pulls us into a space of presence and calm.

'When our women were removed from their land, they weren't able to access the fibres and the river reeds and pass along that skill of weaving,' Carleeta explains. 'But now it's been revived, thanks to our aunties examining the techniques and figuring out the way it was done. So we're still connected, still living and breathing the culture.'

Carleeta's light-blue eyes illuminate when she talks, and it's clear how much this practice means to her. When she's dealing with everyday work and life stresses, she says, she comes out here on Country and all that worry just melts away. Here both she and Cody are emotionally, spiritually and physically stronger. Here, they are connected to their ancestors. Here, they are home.

~

As we drive back to the lighthouse cottage, the sky has turned mauve, and the side of the road is dotted with wombats, wallabies and kangaroos, not all of them alive. Carleeta and Cody stop to move the carcasses of their non-human kin off the road, checking if there are joeys in the pouches, and if any of them are fresh enough to take back to skin and use. Cody is a talented artist – the cottage is strewn with dried wallaby skins, the leather covered in his colourful artworks depicting various creation stories – so he's also keeping an eye out for canvases. In Aboriginal culture, says Cody, nothing goes to waste.

This is what 'caring for Country' really means. Cody and Carleeta look after this whole area as if it were their own backyard. Even though less than 1 per cent of Tasmanian land has been handed back to Aboriginal people, they see it as a place to be cared for, a place you never take too much from and always help to regenerate.

It's inspiring to witness, a potent lesson for us all, and a reminder that even though indigenous peoples make up just 5 per cent of the world's population, they protect a staggering 80 per cent of the planet's biodiversity. Research shows that the world's healthiest, most biodiverse and resilient forests are ones found on land stewarded by indigenous communities. If we want to protect the world's wild places, we must all fight for native lands to be returned to their rightful owners.

~

On our final morning a storm rolls in, vanishing the sun and darkening the sky. Sheets of rain press against the cottage windows, and the sky rumbles and cracks above us. We had a walk planned, and we writers stand around the windows, watching the storm and discussing whether or not to go. But then Carleeta walks in, glances out the window and says no. We will stay inside and string some more shell necklaces instead. 'We take note of things like wind and rain; it's the ancestors telling us it's not the right time.'

There is, of course, a right time for everything in life. A right time to go, and a right time to stay. I think we all know that. Or at least we all have the ability to know that, if we can quiet our conditioned minds, so accustomed to sticking to plans and pushing through no matter how strong the messages are from the natural world, and learn to listen again. We have to listen in a new way, which is actually a very old way, attuning our bodies and brains to heed signs we once all knew how to interpret.

By re-sensitising myself to the land I was born on and learning to listen to it, I have become more aware of what it is asking of me. When the land burned, it was asking me to stay and learn how to look after it better. When disease rampaged across the world, it was asking me to stay very still and quiet, and let all the things I had forgotten return to me. When the water rose, it was asking me once again to stay, and to remember the interconnectedness of us all. Perhaps none of these events were tragedies after all. Perhaps they were all invitations.

The rain does eventually clear. Elli, James and I follow a track through the bush to the bay below the lighthouse, because even though it's mid-winter, James has the mad urge to swim. The sky is still heavy with purple storm clouds. I wander over the boulders on my own, to watch the wind curling over the surface of the water and to breathe the salty air, laced with a whiff of smoke. When I turn to start walking back, bands of sunlight have broken through the clouds, turning the lichen-coloured boulders the colour of a ripe mandarin.

It is time to go.

Part Three

Going

14

Leopard

Rewilding in Rajasthan

A friend of ours passed away in January this year, in the middle of summer, when a Covid wave crashing through our region swept him away with it. He was a prominent Australian artist and a powerful force for good in our community, and his funeral was held on his land, high on a hill. We celebrated a life lived to the fullest. His body was laid out in front of the gathering, covered in sunflowers and overlooking the bush below. His curly golden hair caught the sunlight as his partner spoke to us about love and purpose and passion. 'Ask yourself: are you living the life you want to live?' he said as two black cockatoos circled overhead and goosebumps surged across my forearms.

We must not put things off for another day, our group of friends agreed after the ceremony, as we hugged and cried and danced to Sister Sledge's 'We Are Family', then wrote love notes to our friend and placed them in his coffin. We must not put things off for another day, because there may not be one. As the Pulitzer Prize–winning author Kathryn Schulz writes in her exquisite memoir about grief and love, *Lost & Found*, 'Loss is a kind of external conscience, urging us to make better use of our finite days.'

When an invitation to an assignment in India arrived, soon after I got home from Tasmania, I decided it was the right time to go. It was the right time to see if I could reconcile my desire to explore the world with my desire to not ruin it. Could I balance out the carbon burn with experiences that not only didn't damage the places I was going to see, but maybe even made them a little bit better?

That remained to be seen. But I trusted myself enough now to know the calls when they came. This was one of them.

~

The day before I fly, I'm anxious. Stressing about whether I've packed lightly enough and whether I've got all my reusables so I can avoid all those awful single-use plastics; stressing about finessing an itinerary that will help me tell stories about sustainability and conservation and travel that uplifts the environment and local people; stressing about wrapping up loose ends with work so I can be present and focused while I'm on the ground. Pete's commented a few times that I'm not the 'travel Nina' he remembers, that it never used to make me this anxious. I tell him of course I'm not the Nina he remembers. I'm different now. The world is different now. Everything carries so much more weight.

I want to do this trip the right way. I've decided to only travel overseas once or twice a year from now on, staying for longer periods of time when I do, which means I want to make the very most of every day. And after releasing *Go Lightly* last year, and spending much of the past eighteen months writing articles and recording podcasts and giving interviews on how to travel in a way that conserves more than it destroys, I want to stay accountable.

Twenty-four hours before I fly, I sit in a tea ceremony for a friend's birthday. These are offered weekly in a few venues in our town, which is a bit of a spiritual hub, and I often attend them when the wheels feel like they're falling off. Today, as I sit and watch the tea bowls being cleaned and the water being poured and the steam rising and the incense smoke curling, as I sip the tea and let the earthy brew slide down into my body, I set some intentions for the month ahead. I will try to stay present. I will try to make a difference, however small. I will have fun, goddammit, and remember that to travel this far is one of the greatest privileges we humans have.

~

We come to India, many of us, to have our buttons pushed so we can learn about ourselves. We've heard that it's a place that will delight us as much as it will infuriate us, that it will kiss us only to turn around and slap us in the face a moment later. We seek this extreme volatility because we understand, or at least *want* to understand, that it is the stuff of life. And if we can come to grips with the inevitability of these ups and downs, and learn to accept them whenever they arrive, perhaps we can find some sort of peace.

This was at least part of the reason Pete and I decided to spend that year in India. This time, though, there is very little button-pushing, and my first few days back in the country feel like a blessed kind of homecoming. Like a cord that fell out of its socket has been plugged back in. I arrive in the bustling blue city of Jodhpur with three other Aussie travel writers, two of whom I already know, and the drive to our hotel in a powder-blue tuktuk is a blast of glittering saris, lumbering cows, whizzing motorbikes, beeping horns and high-speed Hindi. I am full of energy and exploding with love for it all.

As soon as I'm back on the ground in this country I've now travelled to four times, I realise how terribly I've missed it. When I get a whiff of that heady mix of incense, spices and manure from the tuktuk, a single tear sneaks down my cheek. I am full of gratitude for being able to reanimate the parts of myself I tucked away when I stopped travelling overseas three years ago.

I am inspired, too, by the progress I see being made here in terms of sustainability. The hotel we're staying in is a glorious light-blue modernist structure that sits at the feet of the city's majestic red sandstone Mehrangarh Fort. This was the first hotel in Rajasthan to go plastic-free. It uses electric tuktuks, grows organic vegetables in a nearby kitchen garden and supports the local community by doing things like cleaning up the neighbouring Toorji Ka Jhalra stepwell. The last time I was in Jodhpur, the

18th-century reservoir was clogged with rubbish and toxic green sludge. Now, though, it is clean and clear. *The future is bright*, I think as I watch local kids dive off the pyramidal steps and into the water, which sparkles in the afternoon light.

~

A morning walk through the old town: roaming ancient indigo-tinged alleyways, ducking beneath ornate Rajasthani archways and side-stepping piles of rubbish and cow poo. An old woman with a hot-pink sari covering her head fills a bucket of water from a communal tap, while an old man with a long white beard and thick moustache sits on the wall opposite, texting on his phone. A cow covered in flies lies beside a rubbish pile, slowly munching an old chip packet, while a merchant with a red sackful of saris thrown over his shoulder yells his sales pitch up to the second-floor houses. Somewhere, someone blasts a Bollywood hit out into the street, and a trio of pigeons flutters down to land on the thick black electricity wires snaking overhead.

The centre of my vision starts to blur. I'm looking at a businessman reading a newspaper, but I can't see his face, only his blue shirt and black pants and bare feet. Whatever I look at directly becomes pixellated by rippling coloured lights, but I can still see peripherally. I'm starting to have an aura migraine.

I've had migraines very occasionally since I was a kid. Both my parents get them too, but lately they've become more frequent. Which I suppose shouldn't come as a surprise, since although no one knows for sure what causes migraines, they tend to show up during times of stress, fatigue and overwhelm. Exactly when you want them the least, in other words.

Auras are strange, almost psychedelic mirages that vibrate, becoming a semicircle that expands outwards from the centre of one side of your vision. Mine usually happen on the left side and last for about twenty minutes, before reaching the edge and dissipating. As the aura expands, it becomes a series of zigzagging patterns, like a kind of Catherine wheel growing across my field of vision. I start to feel a tingling in my face, then my speech can become a little slurred and finding the right words gets hard. I start to feel like I've been pulled out of my own body, and everything – light, noise, smells – becomes more intense. Which, as you can imagine, in India is a lot. It's a bit like a ministroke. The World Health Organization classifies it as equivalent to quadriplegia in terms of the disability caused during an attack.

I put my sunglasses on, sit down in the shade and drink half a bottle of water with two painkillers, since the aura usually precedes acute pain. *Breathe,* I tell myself. *This will pass.* And, of course, with time it does. But it has been a reminder to slow down and listen to my body and what it's asking of me, and to listen to the world around me. I am not the same woman I was three years ago, able to push through jet lag and fatigue and overwhelm without consequence. I have become more sensitive to the world. I am grateful for the memo.

~

It's late afternoon when we arrive at Jawai, in the Godwar region of south-western Rajasthan and a three-hour drive from Jodhpur, the next day. The drive has been madness itself, the road littered with sleeping cows and hurtling hand-painted trucks. But after the bustle of Jodhpur, arriving in a rural area is immediately soothing. I wind down the car window and breathe in the scent of dry dirt and sweet manure. A group of local Rabari, an indigenous tribal caste of nomadic cattle and camel herders, whiz by on motorbikes, with saffron-coloured turbans, white dhoti loincloths and elaborately curled moustaches.

We turn off the highway and onto dirt tracks lined with euphorbia cactus and yellow-flowered Senna trees. Farmers trail herds of buffalo, and village women balance towering bundles of grasses on their heads, as they walk through the honey-coloured afternoon light. Not five minutes from our camp, we turn a corner and there – lying sphinx-like across the crest of a smooth granite outcrop – is a six-foot-long female leopard. Neck extended, paws crossed, Fenella (as we discover she's called) couldn't care less about us or any of the other passers-by.

The three other writers and I peer through binoculars and camera lenses at Fenella, as she scans the horizon with her cool jade eyes. We can hardly believe she's real. It's not long before she slinks off, her spotted tail disappearing over the granite ridge like some kind of mirage.

Seeing a leopard so quickly is, in safari terms, almost unheard of, especially when there are so many people around. But that's exactly what makes the Jawai area, with its population of fifteen thousand people scattered across six hamlets and villages, so unique. The area is home to one of the highest concentrations of leopards on earth, and people have lived here in proximity to leopards for centuries. I've come here to visit a conservation-focused safari camp that's trying to make sure it stays that way.

The camp is owned by an Indian entrepreneur whose family has been in conservation for five generations. Over the nine years since the camp started, they've been working to boost leopard numbers, mostly by replanting former farmland with indigenous scrub and grasses so as to restore habitat and create wildlife corridors. Because of this rewilding, Jawai is now home to twenty-nine adult leopards, up from seventeen leopards six years ago.

To be clear, this isn't the kind of place I could ever afford if I was paying for it with money. It costs upwards of $1200 a night – what I'd usually earn in a (very good) week. Because I'm paying for it with stories, the cost of my stay is covered by the camp, but I don't take one skerrick of the luxury of my tented suite for granted. The last few years have been very tough financially, as I've scrambled to 'pivot' in my career and Pete has tried to get his new business off the ground. It's been a time of tight budgets, of half-filling the petrol tank, of second-hand everything, of swapping and borrowing rather than buying. So to be here now, wafting around this room with its padded white cotton walls decorated with black-and-white prints of leopards, and its rain shower and huge tub in the bathroom, feels particularly decadent.

When the sun starts to set, I follow bush tracks lined with head-high post-monsoon grasses to two open-sided bar and dining-room tents. I wander through billowing white curtains to the courtyard, as the sun drops behind the Aravalli Range, one of the oldest mountain ranges in India. A staff member carefully places flickering lanterns around the courtyard and hangs them in the surrounding neem trees.

We're soon met by a man named Yusuf, the director of wildlife experiences here, dressed in a belted olive-green safari jacket and with a moustache that's as well curled as his British accent is polished. He's like a character from a film. I like him immediately.

We gather around a long table under the stars for a traditional Rajasthani dinner made mostly from food grown in Jawai's organic kitchen gardens, and on the neighbouring farms. Over the meal, Yusuf tells us more about the conservation work going on at this camp. Guests automatically provide a small contribution per person, per night that's put towards conservation activities like replanting indigenous scrub and grasses, opening up caves and den sites that were blocked by farmers, and employing field guides to patrol for poachers. Community development initiatives have also been created, including funding five schools and starting a free mobile medical unit. It's clever because, aside from supporting local communities, the more jobs the camp provides for the community and the more services they offer them, the more invested residents will be in protecting the area's precious flora and fauna.

Back in my room after dinner, I lie on my bed with the lights off, looking out at the night sky and thinking about how this sort of travel experience is really a form of wealth redistribution. People with enough money to pay for these sorts of trips are those who have, statistically, inflicted the greatest damage on the world, and therefore should hold the most responsibility to fix it. The world's richest people are the ones who fly the most, buy the most clothes, eat the most food, drive the most and burn the most fossil fuels, while the world's poorest do the very least of those things. There is a deep injustice to this, of course, because it's the world's poorest who are bearing the brunt of climate change – poverty, migration, hunger, gender inequality and scarce resources. So luring the wealthy in with the promise of the luxury trip of a lifetime, while covertly weaving conservation into it, is genius.

It also helps travellers interact with wildlife the right way, an area I made lots of mistakes in in the past without even realising it. I've ridden elephants in Tanzania and Nepal, and camels in Morocco and India. I went to the circus in Moscow and watched lions perform tricks, and cuddled animals inside zoos and sanctuaries when I should have just left them alone. At the time, I believed I was doing these things because I loved animals and didn't realise how cruel the treatment I was supporting was (except in the case of the circus, when I walked out halfway, in tears). Through writing *Go Lightly*, I discovered that more than half a million animals suffer every day from tourist attractions, though most travellers aren't aware that the animals they're interacting with have been abused, 'broken in' or drugged to make sure they give rides and perform tricks. Thank goodness for living and learning. And thank goodness for camps like this, which help animal-loving travellers actually do a bit of good for the creatures they adore.

~

Early next morning, we head out in a customised safari jeep to see the results of these conservation efforts, the crescent moon and stars still bright in the sky. As we bump along the dusty roads, Yusuf gestures to the forest, explaining that it took two years of rewilding before life started to return. 'Less than a decade ago, this was all under the plough. You never saw a leopard here,' he says, raising his voice over a thrumming chorus of insects.

We complain quietly to each other about the insect snowstorm and pull clear PVC glasses out from the seat pockets in front of us to protect our eyes. But a thriving insect population, though annoying, means a thriving ecosystem. Last year I read the 2015 book *The Moth Snowstorm* by British environment writer Michael McCarthy, which details the loss of the 'moth snowstorm' that used to happen fifty years ago, before the influx of agricultural chemicals. McCarthy describes the moths as 'snowflakes that plastered the headlights and the windscreen until driving became impossible, and you had to stop the car to wipe the glass surfaces clean'. Experiencing this blizzard of insects this morning, then, is a good sign. Perhaps the destruction of nature really can be reversed.

As the sun rises, we pass a small white temple dedicated to the Hindu god Shiva. Along with the three hundred temples and shrines just like it scattered throughout the Jawai region, it's key to conservation, Yusuf explains. The leopard isn't a sacred animal in Hinduism, but because they hang around these temples and shrines, locals associate them with sacredness, and they get a layer of protection. Leopard icons can be found in the temples and, since leopards are considered protectors of their gods, the loss of a goat or sheep is seen as an offering to the gods and the community doesn't take revenge – a perspective that has also helped the leopard population increase. 'Hills that do not have temples and have leopards, the leopards don't tend to survive for very long,' says Yusuf, as we continue driving.

This respectful human and wildlife relationship, along with the camp's rewilding efforts, means you see things here that you won't see elsewhere in the world. Science tells us that leopards are solitary, yet in 2015, says Yusuf, they had sixteen living on the same hill, and four adults sharing the bringing up of cubs. This has never been documented in any scientific study about leopards anywhere else in the world, Yusuf remarks, as we continue driving along a winding sand riverbed. 'There's no logical biological explanation for it, except that the leopards have learned to coexist, knowing that, "We've got this village down there, there's no hope of survival if we don't get along. So why don't we carve out small patches on this hill, and just be nice to each other?"'

As if on cue, a message crackles through the radio that there's a leopard nearby. We hurtle off on a high-speed 'Ferrari safari' to the top of the hill. Behind us is the Jawai Bandh, or dam, created in the 1940s to supply water to Jodhpur. It's now a haven for migratory birds, including cranes from Siberia and flamingos from the western deserts, as well as a healthy population of marsh crocodiles. But the real show is in front of us: two of Fenella's cubs lazing in the sunshine, barely giving us a second glance.

These moments, highlighting the power of rewilding efforts fuelled by tourism, accumulate as my time at the camp ticks on. There's the peacock we see, tail feathers flared, doing an elaborate mating dance for an uninterested peafowl. There's the leopard we almost don't see, just two metres away from our truck, so close one of the other journalists almost ends up in my lap when we realise. There's the male *nilgai*, or blue bull, the largest antelope species in Asia, that we see silhouetted against the night sky on our way back from an early evening game drive.

It's a much smaller thing than all these, though, that really illuminates the benefits of conservation, and of travel when it's done the right way. At some point while watching Fenella's cubs, I look down beside the jeep to see an ashy-crowned sparrow-lark, about 7 centimetres tall, tending its egg-filled nest, which is hidden in a tuft of grass sprouting from a crack in the granite. I point out the nest to Yusuf, who pauses before responding.

'That one lone clump of grass provides all that life support. If you multiply that by all of this,' he says, stretching his arms wide to take in the landscape around us, and the whole wide world beyond it, 'it's a huge potential for regeneration.'

And, indeed, it is.

15

Woman

Weaving a bright future in India

It's 11am in Kaliberi village, and the Saheli Women artisans are hard at work. As I walk out of the beating mid-morning sun into their workshop, a large, cool warehouse space with candy-pink walls, lavender shutters and whirring fans hung from the high ceilings, the dozen or so women are busy at their desks, sewing and hand-stitching and embroidering garments. Wearing bright saris in neon pinks, yellows, oranges, greens and blues, the women are deeply focused, but also laughing and chattering as they work. I'm only half an hour outside of Jodhpur town, where I arrived last night after farewelling the other writers in Jaipur, but I feel as though I've slipped through a portal into another world.

'These women are all Pakistani migrants, and many of them were doing hard labour in mines and cotton fields before this,' says Madhu Vaishnav, the bright-eyed founder of Saheli Women and my host for the week, as she admires the stitching on a blue *ikat* patterned napkin. 'See how beautiful this is?' She lifts the napkin up for me to see. 'My ladies are all doing such good work.'

I discovered Saheli Women, an atelier that has been producing ethically made, sustainable clothes for international fashion brands since 2015, through a designer I interviewed for *Make a Living Living* about five years back. She said Madhu had inspired her to start her successful sustainable fashion business, and was also one of the kindest, most inspired people she knew. When I was organising this trip and looking for regenerative experiences that would give back to local communities, I remembered Madhu and looked her up. Saheli Women, I was excited to discover, had a travel offering – five days immersed with some of their eighty-odd artisans, learning traditional Indian handcraft techniques. I called Madhu immediately.

Madhu gives me an introduction to natural dyeing, pulling big jars of marigold, sappan wood and onion skin powders off the shelves, along with bright rolls of tie-dyed silk that have been coloured with these and other natural pigments. We now consume about eighty billion new pieces of clothing every year, most of which are coloured with toxic chemicals that are often dumped in waterways. Rather than pollute waterways with the harsh chemicals fashion companies usually use, Saheli Women uses natural pigments to colour its fabrics.

While we continue walking around the centre, Madhu, dressed in a deep-pink sari, tells me about the hurdles she had to jump over to start Saheli. They included teaching herself English, convincing her family to let her work as a married woman, fighting to be allowed to travel alone to the University of California, Berkeley, to do a diploma in social welfare as a mother of two young children, then finally starting Saheli with $100 and five women in a centre that at the time had no running water or electricity. Her friends, neighbours and family saw her as very rebellious, cutting her hair short and working for NGOs and travelling overseas for her education. 'I was judged a lot,' she says. 'People thought I was having extramarital affairs, that I was running away from my family, that I would never come back. They felt very sorry for my husband and were giving a lot of sympathy to him.' It was tough, but infinitely worthwhile, she says, as we sit on a colourful woven rug on the concrete floor and share chai and face-scrunchingly sweet *laddus* with the artisans on their tea break.

I think about all the times over the past decade that I've felt judged in a bit of a similar way, by friends and family who've made it clear they thought I shouldn't be leaving Pete quite so often to head off on assignments. More recently, over the past few years, I've felt the judgement from those who've told me I should just chill out and not worry about things so much, because the state of the world isn't my problem. Over time, these judgements do tend to corrode your confidence, no matter how hard you try to ignore them. But meeting Madhu will, I know, help me keep my warrior spirit alive for a long time to come.

'When someone asks me how I describe sustainable fashion, I say this,' says Madhu, gesturing to the women talking and laughing around her, 'fun, free, happy. Every day here is a celebration.' Madhu is passionate about giving the artisans she employs the respect they deserve, and a voice that is heard, so they're seen as humans and not machines.

Most of the women, she says, never went to school, were married when they were in their early teens and have between three and six children to support. For many, working here was a battle they had to fight with their husbands, who didn't understand why they wanted to change their work or to work outside the home. 'But money talks,' says Madhu. 'The men see the money coming into the households and they can't argue with that.'

Madhu pauses as one of the women speaks to her in high-speed Marwari. 'This woman is saying, when women earn, their children respect them more, and they help the mother with the chores. So they become a very good example for the next generation.'

The ripple effects of women's education and work are huge. It's been proven that the best way to reduce emissions is to educate girls in remote rural areas just like this. With better education, women get married later, have fewer children, contribute more to the economy and are better equipped to deal with the climate emergency.

The women soon become inquisitive about me. Where are you from? they ask me with Madhu's help translating. How old are you? Do you have children? When they discover I'm thirty-eight, the age of a grandmother in rural India, but still childless, they shake their heads and furrow their brows at me in pity.

What, I wonder, must these women think of me? The age of a grandmother, yet traipsing around a foreign country, childless and alone. I wonder what they'd make of it if I said that this independence is what I have fought for my entire adult life up until now. That all I ever wanted, for a long time, was to see the world and be free. That having a baby is something I still don't know if I want, at least more than other things – a flourishing career, a deep knowledge of the world, endless time to read and to write and to think about how to help solve the world's most pressing problems. I don't know for sure, but given their pitying looks, I don't think that I can make these ideas of 'freedom' and 'ambition' sound anything other than ludicrous and impossibly selfish.

Instead of trying to convey all this, I shift the conversation to the power of money.

Madhu tells me that the money the women are making here has also been hugely beneficial to their health. 'When you're living in poverty, it's hard to follow a healthy diet, and again I realised the solution was financial empowerment,' she says. 'We can give them medication, but how long can we keep giving that medication? The problem has to be treated at the root. Now, all these ladies have enough money to buy better-quality food, and they are healthy and happy.'

Financial empowerment extends beyond the women's own families, too. Because their households now have more money, they are spending more at the grocery store and the vegetable market, and because of that, more businesses are opening in the village. Everyone wins.

Aside from developing the women's skillsets and paying them a good living wage, Saheli is also inadvertently teaching these women about sustainability. 'This lady here,' says Madhu, translating for a beautiful woman in a canary-yellow sari, 'she says we buy clothes, and if they get dirty or torn, we just throw them into landfill. She says in so many ways we are a burden to the earth, and it handles that with a lot of happiness, so we need to bow to the earth for doing that.'

In a world where we're acutely aware of fashion's carbon footprint, environmental offences and atrocious human rights violations, it feels important to be here and see these women spending an entire day stitching a single garment. I understand so much more now about what this work means for them, their families and their entire village. It's only day one, and I know I'll never wear a piece of clothing without feeling the presence of the human who created it again.

~

The next morning, at Madhu's house in a walled estate outside Jodhpur's indigo-washed old town, Madhu teaches me to grind spices for chai, and to make pan-fried *paratha* flatbreads stuffed with tomatoes, onion, chilli and spices. Before we leave for the day, she shows me the small shrine where her family worships each morning, set with figurines of the Hindu deity Krishna, as well as candles, incense and photos of her family's ancestors. I've travelled to Jodhpur twice before but have never explored outside the main tourist area. Being immersed in a local's life like this feels like peering behind a curtain.

Today Madhu drives us north to the small village of Bhikamkor on the edge of the Thar Desert, to Saheli's other workshop. For women to drive alone is almost unheard of here, and when we pull up at a set of traffic lights, a police officer strolls up to the car, knocks on the window, stares at us for a long minute and asks where we're going and why. Madhu answers him, stony-faced, and after another thirty seconds of mute staring, he finally waves us on.

The drive takes more than ninety minutes, and on the way, Madhu tells me more about the women artisans. Some of them are Dalits, or 'untouchables', the lowest and most repressed caste in India, who, she explains, are usually only allowed to do menial jobs – cleaning toilets, sweeping floors, that sort of thing. Madhu has fought to have Dalits working on garments inside the centre. This is a big deal in rural India, where the 3000-year-old caste system is still very much a part of everyday life. She also has Brahmins, the highest caste, working at Saheli, some of whom she says initially refused to work alongside Dalits. 'I told them, here we are all equal. If you won't work with them, then you can leave now.' Madhu dreams of seeing a society without divisions, and this is her small way of making that a reality.

Soon we arrive at the workshop. It sits on a dirt road where a few long-horned cows and scrappy chickens are foraging for food. It is surrounded by simple village houses and some majestic temple ruins. This centre was once Madhu's husband's grandmother's home, and ever since she first visited, she has dreamt of bringing cotton handlooms back to the village. Handloom weaving is an important art for Indian people, but it's rare now because of fast fashion, says Madhu as we walk through the indigo gates.

Fast fashion is, I've learned from past travels, decimating the continuation of traditional handcraft techniques all over the world. Four years back I travelled to Guatemala to write about a week-long weaving workshop, where I followed the technique of creating the riotously coloured traditional embroidered *huipil* blouses. I learned to spin raw cotton, colour it using natural dyes, then weave it with women who had dedicated their whole lives to the craft. It was a beautiful process with rich history and craftsmanship and tradition, but it's a practice that is dying. A *huipil* can take up to two months to create, and since there are now 15 tonnes of cheap, second-hand clothes being sent to Guatemala from America every month, the younger generation don't want to spend the time and money weaving something when they can just buy a T-shirt for a dollar. Every time I look at the vintage *huipiles* I bought on that trip, now hanging on the walls of our house, I think of the importance of keeping these textile traditions alive and honouring the garments we put on our bodies every day.

Last week, Saheli Women was finally able to buy a handloom, and today the artisans will learn to use it. Their excitement is palpable as they gather around the loom. They watch a smiley young man they call 'masterji', a master weaver and one of the few men allowed inside the centre, show them how to toss the wooden shuttle back and forth between hundreds of colourful cotton threads. When the first few rows are done, the women all clap and laugh and chatter amongst themselves, then we all gather in the main room to celebrate with *laddus* and little cakes and samosas.

I spend the rest of the day learning from the women, trying rather unsuccessfully to use the handloom, embroidering a small square of fabric and hearing more of the women's stories. I watch the women working together, stitching and chatting, children occasionally running in to talk to their mothers. A deep sense of community has been created here. The women come here to earn and to learn, yes, but they also come to see their friends and to complain to each other and to uplift each other. I look around the airy atelier, full of all that colour and laughter, and think, *We are so much stronger together than we are apart.*

The real magic, though, begins at sundown, when Madhu takes me out to visit her family's organic farm. There we pick lentils and sesame seeds and melons, and we cuddle a four-day-old goat. Madhu tells me her dream of one day turning this land into an organic cotton farm, so her business can become completely self-sustaining.

When we return to the village, we visit one of the artisans' homes for dinner. We sit on the floor in a central courtyard in the day's last light, eating some of the best food I've had in India with our hands. Afterwards, Madhu's husband and one of the other male villagers carry two traditional Indian *charpoy* woven beds up to the rooftop of the centre, and, once they leave, Madhu and I are joined by six of the artisans and four of their daughters. We all cram onto the beds, looking at the stars and at the few village lights below, the women gossiping in Marwari, the girls laughing (at me, mostly) and asking endless questions until I fall asleep in my clothes.

We wake at dawn and watch the sun rise over the desert, then the little girls return to braid my hair and make chai. Today is the first day of Navaratri, an annual ten-day Hindu festival devoted to Durga, the mother goddess, and honouring the divine feminine. It seems perfectly fitting to be spending the day with these women, cleaning the centre together, working the handloom and sorting vintage fabrics while I try not to cry from the loveliness of it all.

Throughout the day, the women take turns grabbing my hand and leading me down the dirt tracks snaking off from the centre to show me their homes. The three young daughters of the manager of the Bhikamkor centre take me to their house, set in the ruins of an old mansion, where they feed me slices of melon from their garden and introduce me to their buffalo. Down the road at another artisan's home, I'm ushered into a shaded courtyard to watch a Bollywood film and eat masala crisps, while the artisan oils and plaits her daughter's waist-length hair. To be given this insight into daily life in a village where few tourists would ever come, and to be shown these kindnesses by people who have very little, feels like the greatest luxury of all.

I think, all through the day, of the ways I can give back to Madhu and her artisans once I get back home. Aside from writing travel stories about the important work they're doing and spreading the word on social media, I hope Madhu and I will keep in touch and build a relationship that will continue for years or decades to come, so I can know if there's anything she or the women need, and send potential collaborators her way.

When the shadows start to lengthen, I return to the centre, and Madhu ushers me out into the courtyard and into a small temple. It's dedicated to Durga, and the interior is painted baby pink, like the inside of a seashell. A ninety-year-old Rajasthani woman with beautifully wrinkled skin sings and bangs an Indian *tabla* drum, and one of the artisans sits cross-legged on the ground, rocking back and forth with her eyes closed. I sit in front of a small fire below an image of Durga, letting the hypnotic music reverberate through my bones.

Soon, the pace of the drumming increases, and with it the artisan's rocking. She starts muttering in dialect, louder and louder, until she's yelling out over the drum and slapping her hands against the bare ground. Madhu walks in, takes the water vessel from in front of the Durga statue and starts flicking the holy water in the woman's face, whispering in her ears and rubbing her back to calm her down. A minute later the artisan stands to walk outside with Madhu, but when I go to do the same, Madhu stops me at the door. 'You stay, you pray for your baby,' she says, holding my hand and looking directly into my eyes. She turns and walks away, and I have no other option but to sit back down and do what I've been told.

The 'prayers', such as they are for an agnostic like me, begin to form in my mind. But they are not for my unborn baby. They are for the women here, for women everywhere, for all of us trying to survive and trying to do a bit of good and trying to find joy, during this one fleeting moment we're given on Planet Earth.

There is nothing left to do, then, but bow my head in gratitude.

~

The seatbelt-less taxi careens through the night along a serpentine single-lane road, towards oncoming trucks and sleeping cows and the odd house-sized boulder. The Himalayas soar above me on the left, while to my right yawns a cavernous valley. This morning, I flew from Jodhpur to Rishikesh. It's a ninety-minute drive from the cacophonous yoga capital of Rishikesh to Devprayag, where I am headed, and every hair-raising minute feels like an hour.

Soon, though, I'm able to stop penning mental farewell notes to Pete as my suitcase and I are deposited at the end of a quiet laneway at the entrance to Mandala Retreat Home, where I'll be spending the next four nights. The five-bedroom biscuit-coloured house, set in a mango grove, is as secretive as a pirate's map. Inside, there are rendered walls painted earthy shades of cream, exposed beams hung with gently whirring ceiling fans, a few elegant pieces of hand-carved dark wooden furniture and the odd clay sculpture of a Hindu deity. The overall look is one of Zen simplicity and, after the sensory overload of the last two weeks, it makes me immediately feel Zen, too.

~

The last time I came here – or at least the last time I came to Rishikesh, which was seven years ago now – I did not arrive feeling Zen. Far from it. I arrived in the place where the Beatles famously found enlightenment in tears, sobbing into my open palms, and so very far from the gentle Bodhisattva I'd hoped to present as when I arrived.

I'd taken an overnight bus from Pushkar, another of India's most holy cities, where I'd spent a week practising yoga and meditation and meeting fellow seekers with names like Bird and Fern. The bus was a dinted, coughing, wheezing lump of a thing, but it was cheap, and I had a bench seat to myself and a playlist of Indian ragas to listen to, so I was happy. As we pulled out of the terminus, the fat, ginger sun was dropping below the distant Aravalli Range, drizzling honey over the landscape and filling me with such contentment that the scene started to blur with tears.

Slowly, though, things had started to change. As the light leaked out of the sky and the dark took over, the bus began to fill. At each stop another handful of locals would get on, each of them stacking suitcases and cardboard boxes and cages of chickens higher and higher on top of the bus. My bench seat for two had three of us on it, then four, and once all the seats were jammed, the floor filled too, with dozens of bodies crammed into every spare inch.

I breathed deeply, pushed my scarf between my head and the rattling window and attempted to doze. It was a largely futile endeavour, and by the time I stepped off the bus into a dusty car park at dawn, I'd barely managed to snatch one hour's sleep. The bus driver introduced me to a tuktuk driver who, he promised, would take me directly to the ashram I was heading for. I asked the driver, twice, if he *definitely* knew where the ashram was. 'Of course, madam,' he replied with a dismissive head wobble, then proceeded to drop me in town instead.

Rishikesh is divided in two by the mighty Ganges River. I, of course, found myself on the wrong side of the river, so I then had to lug my swollen suitcase across a 2-metre-wide suspension bridge. By then, only about 8am, it was already 40 degrees, and the bridge was crammed with motorbikes, beggars, locals, tourists and cows. I reached the other side, my white shirt soaked through with sweat, only to be told I'd have to take a seven-minute taxi ride to the ashram – one that would cost more than my ticket for the overnight bus. And with that news came the tears.

The young Indian man who had quoted me the price implored me not to cry. When I told him I couldn't help it, that I felt exhausted and heat-addled and swindled, he wobbled his head pityingly and told me, 'It is good you are visiting this ashram, madam, it will be of great help to you.' He was right, of course, but I wanted to pinch him.

I remember all of this as I settle into Mandala – relatively calmly and patiently, despite the terrifying taxi ride – and I feel grateful for growing older and perhaps even a bit wiser. It's 11pm by now but the manager insists I eat a bowl of sweet-corn soup, then take a glass of lemongrass tea to bed, which is in one of the two thatched-roof earthen cottages in the property's gardens. When I finally reach the cottage, I barely make it inside before passing out on the bed from exhaustion.

~

My first morning at Mandala, I wake hours later than I usually would, my body heavy with sleep. Pulling the curtains aside, I'm greeted by views of the thickly forested Himalayas. I climb back into bed to read the retreat's small guidebook. 'Mandala is not a hotel, but a destination for new beginnings,' it reads, 'a place to practice rituals that blossom consciousness and remind us of who we are.'

I've visited a handful of retreats for work over the years, and more often than not find that the daily schedules packed with 'wellness' experiences leave me feeling as though I need a holiday from the supposed holiday. The offer here, though, is time and space to build your own practices and rituals. The little booklet is filled with ideas, from sitting and breathing, or repeating mantras, to drinking tea mindfully, or just watching the cows in the street. I can hardly think of anything more delightful, or more needed, than to give myself time and space to digest the journey so far.

Up in the communal lounge in the main house, where floor-to-ceiling glass windows overlook the Himalayas and singing bowls adorn the low wooden coffee table, a steaming pot of chai and freshly baked cookies beckon from the kitchen bench. Two other guests are arriving this afternoon, but for now it's just me, which allows me the illusion that I have unearthed this place, that it is my secret. I carry a cup of chai into the adjoining courtyard and sit beside the pool, overlooked by a Buddha statue, to do as the guidebook suggested and write in my journal. Mandala is intentionally wi-fi-free, to support contemplation and deep rest, and I already feel a shawl of calm being thrown over my shoulders.

Soon, though, I'm joined by the manager, a striking Indian woman dressed in an elegant dusky-pink kurta pyjama set with short silver hair, dark eye makeup and a manner of speaking so serene it almost sends me back to sleep. 'Anyone who enters here is changed,' she half-whispers when I tell her how relaxed this house makes me feel. 'You can really feel the energy of this place.'

She attributes this energy to the fact that before the house became a retreat in late 2019, it was inhabited for fifteen years by a sadhu, or Hindu holy man, who spent much of his time here meditating in silence, infusing it with his blessings and peaceful energy.

Devprayag and the surrounding Himalayan mountains have been inhabited by mystics and sages for centuries, since it's set at the confluence of two revered rivers – the roaring jade-coloured Bhāgīrathī and the sluggish, chocolate-hued Alaknanda. The two rivers combine at this exact point to become the sacred Ganges River. This, it's said, infuses the town of Devprayag with a potent spiritual energy, since Indians consider the Ganges to be the mother of the country, and the personification of the *shakti* life force energy inside us all.

Many of these holy men spend their lives meditating in caves in the surrounding mountains, which are also dotted with temples and shrines. After a second chai, I take a walk to a local temple, set on a hill with 360-degree views of the Himalayas. It's still Navaratri, and I arrive just in time to witness a small ceremony, where a local priest chants and offers incense and butter lamps to a statue of Durga.

In spiritual terms, I find I gain just as much from lazing by Mandala's pool, from watching red-billed blue magpies swoop through the mango trees, and from sitting quietly and observing the river on Mandala's private beach. The river is a rich brown, coloured by sediment that has been agitated by the constant churning of the water as it surges downstream.

As I lie there on the beach, eyes closed and back pressed against the warm granite, listening to the rush of the water and breathing in its mineral scent, an old familiar sense of guilt starts to whisper in my ear.

Don't forget, it says, *we are in a time of crisis. This is not a time for rest. This is time for action.* The longer I lie there and think about it, though, the more I understand that urgent times do in fact call for quietude. They call for rest and recovery, and even for pleasure, so we can return to ourselves and find that sense of amazement and curiosity that ultimately keeps all of us going. It's also important so we can get in touch with the big, bold, creative ideas that just might help save the world, which will never get airtime if our heads are crammed full of to-do lists.

This thought arises again later by the river, when we meet – me, the two other guests and Mandala's mindfulness teacher – for a sunset ritual. We're instructed by our teacher, another striking woman who used to teach mindfulness at schools in Delhi, to sit on a pebbly platform next to the river and breathe for a few minutes. Then we are to choose five pebbles, holding them one by one and repeating a mantra for each of the five elements – 'I am earth, I am strong and grounded', for example; 'I am water, I have clarity'; 'I am air, I am in flow'. I hold each of the pebbles, and I do feel myself connecting more deeply to the elements.

Finally, we're asked to set a silent intention for the days ahead, and I immediately know what mine is. *Surrender.* I know that letting go and allowing things to just be will help me make the most of the two weeks I have left in this part of the world. And that slowness and deep rest are exactly what I need.

Devprayag town beckons early the next morning. I take the fifteen-minute walk there. Shops selling tea, incense and prayer beads line the steep, narrow alleyways, which are full of rusted bicycles, scraggly stray dogs and skinny cows. Candy-coloured houses and ancient temples cling to the sides of the mountains. Below them Hindu pilgrims and sadhus gather on the banks of the sacred confluence. The Ganges is able to purify all manner of sins, Hindus believe, and facilitate liberation from an eternal cycle of life and death. Everyone is dunking themselves in the holy water, a swirl of jade and brown, as the two waterways blend to form one of the world's most mighty rivers.

I sit and watch the water, reflecting on what it means to merge the disparate forces inside me – inside us all. To unite, to combine, to blend. The last few years, that deep current of silence and stillness has floated so many unexpected gifts into my life. And now here I am, somewhere upstream, and so far from where I began. Trying to merge that quiet with the quick of being out in the world, trying to integrate all of those lessons as I move about the planet again, and trying to make sense of it all.

The green and amber waters beneath me aren't merging seamlessly, they're crashing and bashing into each other and making whirlpools and eddies as they do. It's roaring and chaotic and messy. The pilgrims and sadhus need to clutch on to thick chains hanging from the banks to stop themselves getting sucked away by that combining force. My merging isn't smooth either. I can already feel the vortex my re-emergence into the wider world is creating inside my body, and I also want to hang on to a safety cable so I don't get swept away by the force of it. But all I can do, *all I can do*, is let the vortex be. Until at some point further upstream, I find a more gentle flow.

~

'Tune in', reads one of the directives from the Mandala booklet. 'We have been habitually trained away from the practice of noticing the energetics of the external environment. Learn to follow your feelings in relationship to space.' I'm not exactly sure what that means, but I take it as a permission slip, and when I return to Mandala I drain half the day away inside my cottage, meditating and journalling and napping. Trying to let go of the 'shoulds' I always have catalogued in my head when I'm travelling.

Eventually, the voice telling me there's something better I should be doing with my time intensifies. Maybe I should walk into town again. Maybe there's a hike I should be doing. Maybe I should tether onto the manager's phone to use the Internet to check my emails and post on Instagram. Maybe I should write to Pete and ask him to join me because I think he could be lonely. Actually, I think *I* could be lonely.

To quiet the voice, I wander down to the river and sit in the sunshine with my back pushed up against the same boulder as yesterday, watching the water rush by below me and trying to get my brain to mimic its flow. Eventually, it works. Eventually, I remember the lesson that life has been thumping me over the head with for the past three years. That Vipassana, that the mushrooms, that the garden, that all of it has been trying to tell me: that life reveals the best of itself to us when we are still. And that sometimes, the most urgent thing of all is to simply stop and do nothing at all.

16

Mountain

Seeking wisdom in the Nepalese Himalayas

The first time I learned about The Happy House was in an article I read three years ago by one of my favourite travel writers, a British woman named Sophy Roberts. I had followed Roberts' writing closely for years and had become, for want of a better word, a fangirl. Her story was so deliciously evocative and made The Happy House sound so close to a truly regenerative travel experience, that I vowed it would be one of the first places I'd visit when I eventually travelled overseas again.

So when I step off the helicopter in the small Himalayan village of Phaplu, a thirty-minute flight from Kathmandu in north-eastern Nepal's remote Solukhumbu district, and find Roberts waiting to get on that very helicopter, I take it as a sign. I am exactly where I'm meant to be.

Stay cool, I tell myself, then walk straight up to her and blurt, 'You're Sophy Roberts!' as though she may have forgotten. She, in contrast, is grace personified, whispering conspiratorially to a staff member, 'Take special care of her, won't you,' before darting off to the chopper, blonde hair flying. Then just like that, just like a dream, she is gone.

I had wanted to travel to The Happy House overland from India, but discovered that the drive would take forty-two hours. On this particular trip, I sadly didn't have a week to spare for my Greta Thunberg moment, and so opted for the thirty-minute helicopter ride from Kathmandu. We skimmed over terraced green mountains, past waterfalls and clusters of tiny rural villages, eventually landing on the remote airstrip surrounded by snow-capped peaks.

I walk with a Sherpa guide and four other travellers for five minutes through Phaplu, a collection of small shops and simple houses, until we reach The Happy House. The traditional stacked-stone Sherpa house sits at the end of a long stone pathway, lined with towering pines and prayer flags snapping in the crisp wind. Thanks to Sophy's story, I know Sir Edmund Hillary rented this house occasionally over an almost thirty-year period while overseeing his Himalayan Trust projects and called it his 'happy house' – hence the name. I also know that the explorer and author Levison Wood has recently stayed here. This recovering world traveller feels inordinately lucky to be here.

On the sprawling front lawn we're greeted by Ang Tshering, the handsome, softly spoken, 33-year-old grandson of the original owner, who now runs the show here. The Happy House was originally built by Ang's grandfather, then upgraded by an Italian named Count Guido Monzino. In 1973, Monzino led the first Italian expedition to Mount Everest with the help of more than six thousand porters and guides carrying everything including gambling tables, sofas and silver service. He passed through Phaplu during this expedition and fell in love with it, and when he met Ang's grandfather, he offered to upgrade his house in exchange for making it his part-time abode. The result of this collaboration is a space that feels as much like a film set as it does a Buddhist monastery.

Ang welcomes us into the combined lounge and dining room, where colourful Buddhist *thangka* paintings, depicting Buddhist gods and demons that are meditations to both create and behold, adorn every wall and beam. Hand-sewn Tibetan curtains cover the doorways; pendant lamps hang low over the dining table; Nepalese masks, figurines of deities and guttering butter lamps line the shelves. The overall effect is equal parts reverential, celebratory and homely. I can't imagine anywhere else in the world I'd rather be.

We eat brunch under wide white umbrellas on the lawn, a parade of traditional Nepali dishes, including morel mushrooms and tendrils of young tree ferns plucked from a nearby forest. Then we spend the afternoon acclimatising.

The Happy House needed to be almost completely rebuilt and reinforced following Nepal's devastating 2015 earthquake, which killed almost nine thousand people. Nepal's history is rife with these sorts of hardships – civil war, natural disasters, fuel shortages, border clashes and poverty. Yet no matter where I've gone on my three trips to the country so far, the locals seem unfailingly optimistic. Always ready with a smile and a laugh, always wanting to help and to give.

Perhaps this positive attitude stems from the Buddhist beliefs that infuse this part of the country, I think, as I study the *thangka* paintings in the lounge. I stop at the wheel of life, a mandala representing the foundational Buddhist concepts of karma, nirvana and rebirth. At the bottom of the wheel is a depiction of hell, all fire and demons and darkness and suffering. At the top, an interpretation of heaven, with clouds and gods and sunlight and lush landscapes. We, of course, live in the middle, and everything we do dictates in which direction we will eventually go. Maybe living life underpinned by the belief that our actions all mean something, that they will help us to either rise up to the heavens or descend down through hell, is a very good thing. Maybe we could all benefit from believing that moral behaviour and calm, mindful living in this life will enhance our experience of the next.

~

The following morning, we hike for three hours up through steep rhododendron forests dotted with waterfalls and thickets of wild raspberries, our two Sherpa guides collecting rubbish from the track as we go. The Sherpa people, who originally migrated here from Tibet five hundred years ago, regard the Solukhumbu region as a *Beyul* or sacred valley. Watching them treat the land with reverence and respect is a reminder of what good stewardship looks like.

While we walk higher into the mountains, Ang tells me about the violent civil war that ravaged Nepal for a decade from 1996, killing seventeen thousand people. On a winter's night in 2001, the war's biggest battle broke out around Phaplu. Ang's mother and his father, who was the mayor of Solukhumbu at the time, spent a night hiding under the floors of The Happy House, while the Maoists shot and killed more than three hundred people, including thirty-five government officials. The next morning Ang's parents fled to Kathmandu, and twelve days later migrated to the US where they'd been given political asylum. 'My mother has never come back to Nepal,' says Ang, walking two metres ahead of me.

It's a devastation I can hardly imagine, and yet Ang seems at peace with it. Maybe it's because so much time has passed, or maybe it's because of his Buddhist mindset, I think, as we arrive at Chiwong monastery. Built by Ang's great-great-great-grandfather in 1923, the monastery clings dramatically to a cliff edge, surrounded by a tumble of pine-crusted mountains. I'm sweating and panting with effort, but I can't stop smiling as I receive a welcome blessing from one of the saffron-robed monks, who drapes a white *khata* ceremonial scarf around my neck. Dozens of the other fifty-seven monks who live here gather around, most of them children, to welcome us with shy giggles and pressed-palm namastes. They watch us from the corners of their eyes as we sit at a table in the central courtyard and are served a deliciously simple lunch, and as we're shown around their temple.

On the hike back down we pass *mani* stones, boulders higher than our heads carved with devotional mantras that are a call to awareness for trekkers. We also pass stupas strung with prayer flags in the colours of the five elements – yellow for earth, green for water, red for fire, white for air and blue for sky. These flags are believed to absorb compassion and goodwill, and then with each flutter radiate it out into the world. I stand beneath them, eyes closed, listening to their snapping. When I can't sleep, I often listen to podcasts by one of my favourite Buddhist teachers, Tara Brach, in which she often talks about feeling 'the curve of a smile' spreading through the belly, through the heart. It's always seemed too abstract for me; I just couldn't envisage it. Today, though, I can. Today I imagine a smile bending up through my torso, through my head, lifting up into the sky above. The past few years have been shattering in so many ways, but just look where they've brought me.

It is as fulfilling a travel day as I can remember and, hungry for more, I plan a hike up to their ridgetop camp the following day. The capricious Himalayas, however, have other plans. A storm arrives overnight, bringing with it thick mist and heavy rain, and I have no choice but to bunker down at The Happy House. 'We Sherpas never make plans,' says Ang over breakfast, when I lament my foiled plans. 'Everything just happens as it happens.'

I spend the day adopting the Sherpa mindset, reading books about Himalayan architecture and Tibetan Buddhism, sipping tea laced with house-made honey while wrapped in thick blankets, and chatting with Ang about the good work he and his Sherpa team are doing thanks to the money coming in from this hotel: the mountain bikes they are providing to local kids to encourage them to stay in school; the smokeless stoves they are distributing to homes in the area, since open-fire cooking is the leading cause of death in kids here; the funds they are giving the local Phaplu hospital and Chiwong monastery.

This, I'm reminded, is why it's so important travellers choose where we stay carefully. According to the UN's World Tourism Organization, just 5 per cent of money spent by us travellers actually stays in the communities we visit, with the rest leaking out into the pockets of multinational corporations. One of the best ways to plug these leaks is to support small, locally owned businesses like Ang's, so we can use our hard-earned travel dollars to fund them and the communities and projects they support.

~

The rain hasn't disappeared by morning, but it has eased enough for a Sherpa named Tshering (this is a common Sherpa name, meaning 'long life' in Tibetan) and me to head out on an overnight adventure. Heaving big, covered packs onto our backs and popping umbrellas up over our heads, we step out into the misty morning and start walking. The chilly air smells of sap and clean wood. The paths that burrow through the forest and drop down into the valley below are slippery. We walk through small villages, where dripping washing hangs outside rammed earth houses with blue and red tin roofs. There are friendly, fluffy-tailed mountain dogs sleeping out the front, and a buffalo or goat in almost every garden. Every house grows food to eat – corn or spinach, chillies or sesame seeds, sometimes all of it at once.

We walk for hours and hours, thick clouds of mist muffling everything. Mostly, we walk in silence. Sometimes, though, Tshering breaks out into exuberant stories about growing up here, where he had to walk four hours a day to and from school and learned to run in a zigzag to get away from bears. Every so often we stop to snack on nuts and Snickers bars, or sit in wooden tea houses clinging to the sides of the mountains to drink sugary tea and slurp hot, salty noodle soup. A roaring river, full to bursting at the end of the rainy season, follows us most of the way. We crisscross it using narrow bridges hung with dozens of strings of prayer flags. Ancient stupas with huge eyes painted on them, representing the all-seeing eyes of the Buddha, overlook the mountains.

After five hours of hiking, we arrive at Thupten Chöling monastery at the top of a steep ascent. The monastery was started on donated land in 1968 after Trulshik Rinpoche, a highly respected lama who was one of the Dalai Lama's primary teachers, and some of his followers fled here from Tibet following the Chinese invasion. Today, around nine hundred monks and nuns, 80 per cent of them Tibetan refugees, call Thupten Chöling home.

We're escorted into the grounds by a teenage monk, who leads us up past the small nuns' and monks' houses tumbling down the hillside to the guesthouse where we and any other pilgrims will be spending the night. Our rooms are bare-bones simple, nothing more than a bed and a window. We have just enough time to throw our bags down, wash our hands and change our T-shirts before Tshering ushers me off to the evening ceremony.

Up the hill is a cavernous hall, the doorway hung with Tibetan curtains and the inside painted with colourful *thangka* paintings, just like at The Happy House. We sit quietly on pillows up the back, watching dozens of nuns shuffle in in their maroon robes. They steal glances at me and offer namastes and smiles, then take their seats on the floor on low maroon cushions. Soon, the chanting begins, the nuns reading from ancient prayer books balanced on small wooden chairs in front of them.

The hall fills with sound – the droning of Tibetan horns, the clanging of cymbals, the slow tolling of drums and the deep wail of their chanting. Every so often they wave their hands in unison, their fingers poised in a symbolic mudra, or they all ring a small bell, making the kind of sound you might hear in a Disney movie when a fairy appears. A few helpers walk slowly down the rows with enormous silver urns of salted butter tea or sweet chai. The nuns unwrap small maroon bowls from their cotton coverings and offer them up for the tea, and, when they're done drinking, they lick the bowls like cats before wrapping them back up again.

As I watch the nuns, I daydream about what it would be like if I stayed here and donned the maroon robes myself. If I devoted my life to praying and chanting and meditating for the happiness of all beings. If I left all my worldly possessions behind, if I left Pete and Milka and our home behind and floated free in this oasis of calm, so far away from the mad churn of the outside world. The peace the nuns' rhythms and rituals are projecting out into the world is good and necessary. The longer I think about it, though, the more I'm sure that my role on Earth isn't this one. Not now, anyway. Being far away from home has made it clearer than ever: for now, I must be out in the world. There is work to be done.

~

I'm woken just before dawn, after a very long and peaceful sleep, and head back to the hall for another ceremony. This morning, while the monks and nuns chant, elaborate Buddhist statues called *tormas*, made of flour and coloured butter, are paraded around the hall, then taken outside and left on benches for the dogs and crows to eat. It's a reminder of the impermanence of all things. *Nothing lasts*, the voice inside me says. *Not our sorrows or our pains, not our joys either. We must inhabit each moment. We must do good when we can.*

Outside, before we start the long hike back to Phaplu, an old monk with a face peppered with dark age spots walks over and grabs my hands. Looking into my eyes through his glasses, and with Tshering's help translating, he tells me how happy he is that I'm here. He takes a piece of coal from a nearby offering pyre and crouches to write a series of numbers on the stone steps we're standing on. *1959*: the year he escaped Tibet and started living in the forest for years before this monastery was established. *80*: the age he is now. He tells Tshering that this monastery saved his life. He tells me, as if reading my thoughts from last night, that I don't need to wear red robes to feel spirit inside me and to find God. If I want to live a good life, if I want to be at peace, he says, I only have to read a few pages of the Dalai Lama's books first thing every morning. I promise him I will.

~

On my final afternoon in Phaplu, I accompany another guest and a Sherpa up to The Happy House's ridge-top camp for the night. It's a two-hour hike to get there. We cross tousled meadows draped in glittering spiderwebs. Golden afternoon light catches in thickets of purple and white wildflowers, bending their heads in the breeze. When we enter the Magic Forest, the scene becomes shrouded in mist that curls around our bodies and the soaring birch and fir trees, some of them over two hundred years old.

Silence falls over the three of us like a heavy cloak as we walk along, admiring the wild mushrooms popping up from the wet earth, the neon mosses carpeting the ground and the moody lichens hanging over almost every branch. Occasionally, sunlight wriggles slim fingers between the trees, as our Sherpa guide whistles out into the forest, warning bears of our presence. The hike is steep, the ground slippery with moss and mud and pebbles. I have to work hard to push my sweaty body to the top of the slope, but I remind myself that nothing good ever comes without work.

We arrive at camp, set on a cloud-shrouded ridge, as twilight descends. We are greeted with red wine and steaming bowls of Sherpa dumpling soup. We throw our backpacks into our tents, then bunker down by winking candlelight inside the main tent, a round Mongolian *ger* with a small fire blazing in the centre. The view outside has been completely covered by cloud, but we're content to just sit and listen to the Sherpas tell stories about their Everest expeditions. When I fall into my single bed later in the evening, I discover a hot water bottle has been slipped into it, making me warm as toast.

At dawn, I zip the tent flap open and wander down to the *ger*. I'm just in time to see the sky momentarily clear and the distant snow-capped Himalayan peaks emerge. The morning sun ricochets off the snow caps, the crisp mountain air catches in my throat and time stands still for a moment. Then the breeze picks up, the clouds shift and just like that – just like a dream – they are gone.

~

Arriving back in Kathmandu is like being slapped awake after a fainting spell. From the helicopter, I watch as the rumpled Himalayan valleys give way to the claustrophobic urban sprawl, the buildings packed so tightly together that there's hardly a patch of green between them, and I despair about the devastation we humans have caused by creating these choking cities.

When I'm actually down in the choking city, though, I'm reminded of the wondrous things we humans have created inside it. I explore the World Heritage–listed Patan Durbar Square, dotted with dozens of red-brick temples with meticulously carved woodwork and solid gold gilding, and I watch processions of chanting locals dressed in red and white, their necks strung with marigold garlands for Dashain. I have lunch with an Indian friend I made through *Make a Living Living* overlooking one of the most important Buddhist stupas in the world, where monks, old Tibetan women and camera-wielding tourists all worship as one. I find myself in a Buddhist bookshop in the winding alleyways of Thamel and buy a book by the Dalai Lama and, the next day, a small brown clay Buddha statue to go with it. His head will have cracked off by the time

I return home, but I will superglue him back together again and place him on my altar. He will remind me to stay true to my promise to the old monk from the monastery. He will remind me to stay true to myself.

On my final night in Kathmandu, the night before I fly back to Australia, I decide to take myself to the Pashupatinath cremation ghats, on the banks of the sacred Bagmati River. It's a twenty-minute taxi ride through the honk and blare of the city, but I know it will be worth it. When I arrive, I walk down the dusty steps leading to the river, flanked by some of the site's four-hundred-odd shrines. Sadhus wrapped in tangerine blankets with long tangled beards beg for alms and wild macaque monkeys scamper across the scene.

It is a full moon tonight, I notice, as I take my seat on the concrete platform next to the river and watch the large funeral pyre burning on the opposite bank. The side of it is draped in dozens of marigold garlands, and a barefoot attendee stokes the blaze with a long poker, flames leaping high into the night. Soon, the evening *aarti* ceremony begins. Three turmeric-robed priests perform their choreographed ceremony, offering oil lamps shaped like serpents and fistfuls of incense to the river. A priest gives a sermon in Hindi, and the crowd starts to sing and clap along to the chants being blasted out from the speakers beside us. Smoke billows, bells chime. On the opposite side of the river, a corpse wrapped in cotton is being kissed and blessed by loved ones, before being placed in the fire and engulfed by flames.

As I sit there under the full moon, I am filled with a distinct sense of the fragility of life, and of the blip we all are on the long highway of time.

In this moment, I'm more certain than I have ever been that our job here on earth, for the fleeting moment we're inhabiting it, is simply to be good to it. To love it, as fiercely as we can. To remember that everything we do or don't do matters, that every choice we make matters. To learn from our mistakes and to share those learnings with others. And to not let a single moment on earth go by, without being grateful for all of it.

We have all been born into a world whose terms and conditions we never signed up to. A world built on capitalism and consumerism and colonialism that, more often than not, is run by unquenchable greed and a limitless desire to conquer and destroy. But I think about the Buddhist wheel of life, which tells us that despite all that, we actually live in the best of all possible worlds – not in heaven, not in hell, but right here on earth. Where we can, if we choose to, do very good things. Whether you believe in rebirth or nirvana or any of that doesn't matter. The fact is that we have been born at this exact moment in time, when our world is most broken and begging us to stand up for it, precisely because we are capable of doing just that. Every last one of us, imperfectly perfect and with our own unique gifts and talents, which we can use to make our world a better place – or at least to save our own species from extinction.

I look up at the full moon, at the inky sky, at the stars, and I imagine myself up there with them, looking down on the world. Looking down on the Sherpas who have guided me, the monks who have blessed me, the Nepalis and Indians who have offered their kindness and smiles and pressed-palm namastes, and I say thank you. Looking down on the bears and the belugas, the fires and the floods, the mushrooms and the mountains, and I say thank you. Looking down on Country and on the custodians of Country, the rivers and the oceans and the waterfalls, the bugs and the bees and the bird, and I say thank you. Looking down on my mother, on all of our mothers, on Mother Earth, and I say thank you.

I say thank you.

17

Rainbow

Taking action on Heron Island

The midday sun is beating down on Heron Island, a small coral cay at the southern end of the Great Barrier Reef. I'm sitting on a marble-white stretch of sand licked by turquoise waters next to actress Claudia Karvan and model Gemma Ward, sharing stories about how climate change has affected our lives.

It's not your usual Friday afternoon. But then again, this Heron Island Fellowship – a collaboration between Australia's Climate Council and a climate action funding platform called Groundswell – isn't your usual gathering. For the past few years, this event has collected some of Australia's biggest experts in climate, science and First Nations justice together with some of the country's most powerful cultural influencers – actors, musicians, artists, business leaders and activists – to dive deep into the realities of the climate crisis and brainstorm ideas for how to spread the word about the issue. Our group of forty-something fellows also

241

includes an ARIA-winning musician, a Gold Walkley Award–winning photojournalist and a successful fashion designer.

Day one, and we have already been bombarded with alarming and inspiring talks from the expert speakers. Their messages couldn't be clearer. Climate change and its impacts are accelerating. The burning of coal, oil and gas are causing worsening heatwaves, droughts and floods, and will continue doing so unless we take stronger and swifter action. But we are also far more powerful than we think when it comes to pushing for the critical systemic change we need in order to limit the earth's warming.

There is an urgency to the speaker's messages that makes the hairs on the back of my neck stand up. And there's a trio of statistics shared that I know, even if all the other information shared this weekend fades over time, will stay with me. Are you ready?

Two degrees. This is the hard red line we absolutely must stay below if we want to stand a chance of continuing to live on Planet Earth. It's 1.5 degrees ideally, but it looks as though we're due to bust through that quite soon.

575 gigatons. This is the amount of carbon that can be burned before we reach two degrees.

Five. The number of times *more* than that 575 gigatons of carbon that fossil fuel companies have already bought or own for future use.

When those figures are shared, we look around at each other, eyes wide with alarm. We're all, I'm certain, thinking the same thing. We. Are. Screwed. But, we're told, if we get politically active, and start lobbying our government to not burn those carbon stores and start moving towards a clean energy future instead, there may still be hope. The organisers of this event believe it shouldn't be up to individuals to shift their behaviours (although they encourage us to make the least environmentally impactful decisions we can, since consumer choices do influence political manoeuvring), but for governments and powerful corporations to take responsibility and do what's best for citizens, rather than for their back pockets.

The irony of travelling on a jet-fuelled plane to attend a climate crisis mitigation event is not lost on me. But after twenty-four hours on Heron Island, I understand why Groundswell felt the need to bring us here, to show us one of the places we're most in danger of losing if we don't take serious action now. In between sessions in the classroom, we boat out onto a vibrantly healthy section of the Great Barrier Reef to see all that's at stake. I pull on my snorkel and wetsuit and tumble off the side of the boat, and start snorkelling past sleek blacktip reef sharks, soaring manta rays and gigantic green turtles. When I see a small oval-shaped jellyfish wobbling towards me, I turn to swim away from it to avoid getting stung, but as I do, I notice the most extraordinary thing. This jellyfish is covered in rainbows, with pulses of bioluminescent electricity shimmering up and down its body. I pull off my mask and yell out to the group I'm snorkelling with, 'Umm, there's a magical jellyfish over here, you've gotta see it!'

A few of them swim over, and we bob around the flashing creature like gigantic life buoys, until someone points out that there's a tiny iridescent fish living *inside* the jellyfish. As luck would have it, our guide this morning is one of the world's most revered marine scientists – the guy who wrote the oceans section of the Paris Climate Accords – and he tells us this is not actually a jellyfish but a comb jelly, which uses eight rows of comb-like plates to travel underwater. As they swim, their combs break up light and create the rainbow luminescence we're seeing. Comb jellies and the tiny fish that seek shelter inside them, he says, have probably lived in this symbiotic relationship for millions of years, in a perfect example of interdependence. There really isn't another word for it – it is utterly enchanting. I don't stop watching the comb jelly until I hear the last call to get out of the water.

Later, lying on the sand under a casuarina while waiting for our next lesson to start, I can't stop thinking about the comb jelly. Perhaps we all need our climate totems. Some people have whales. Some people have koalas. I now have the magical rainbow comb jelly. I will conjure it every time I think it's too hard to go to that protest, or get political, or buy less plastic packaging, or walk instead of driving, or any of the dozens of important choices I make every week. I'll think of the jellyfish, and I will *do* something. Because I want to live in a world where the ocean isn't too hot for psychedelic rainbow jellyfish to exist. Surely we all want that.

~

Being immersed in all the rich biodiversity we're slowly killing does a good job of enhancing the messages shared by the experts in their talks about climate science and warming impacts, about the political drivers and obstacles for climate action, and about how we can build resilience for a safer future.

The most powerful moments, though, are the ones that unfold on the sand, brainstorming and sharing ideas for how we might contribute to the movement in ways large and small. On day one, I had a few hushed conversations with some of the other fellows about their confusion as to why they had been included. *I don't know anything about the climate crisis. I'm not a scientist. I'm not an activist. What can I possibly do to make a difference?* I felt the same.

By day three, though, things have shifted. Thanks to those group brainstorming sessions, we're realising that the world needs our biggest, brightest, weirdest and wildest ideas. Also, that every one of us has a way of contributing, that we're all powerful in our own ways. We don't all need to be chaining ourselves to bulldozers or joining Extinction Rebellion or becoming climate scientists. We just need to harness whatever talents and skills we have and use them to spread the message to whatever audience we have. Which might be millions of people or might just be our partner or mum or friend. Whether we make art about it or write stories about it or email our MP's office about it or spread awareness on social media or attend rallies and marches or donate to climate action groups or make more sustainable daily choices or start up a conversation with someone about it doesn't matter. What matters is that we do *something*.

The world needs our creative fire, because the world is in dire need of a revolution of the imagination. The old broken systems are being questioned, and we need a collective reimagining of how we power, employ, house and organise ourselves, in order to create infinitely better systems. These brainstorming sessions, filled with delightfully wacky, wild ideas, remind me that we can use our creativity to imagine the world we long for, so we can go out and make it a reality. Sharing ideas for solutions like this has also been proven to reduce eco-anxiety, and taking action definitely helps me feel more positive and purposeful.

That first day on the beach, one of the fellows said something that has become a bit of a mantra for us all. 'Imperfect action is better than perfect inaction.' We're all terrified of not doing things 'perfectly'. Of not knowing enough or doing enough or being influential enough or being as good as that person we just saw saving the world on Instagram. We need to stop thinking like that. As the scientists this weekend have told us, we've got seven years to reduce emissions by 75 per cent below 2005 levels and turn this thing around. Which is to say, we've got seven years to save our own lives. We need all hands on deck to do that.

We can all spend money with the climate in mind, make our daily choices with the climate in mind and help build the movement in whatever way we can. More importantly, we can vote with the climate in mind, and all help push for massive systemic change right now, putting as much pressure as we can on governments to stop burning coal, oil and gas. And most importantly, if you ask me, we can develop a deeper sense of belonging to our shining, terrible, mystifying, absurd, dazzling, imperilled world, so that we can become a more beneficial presence for it and help bring it back to life. We have to stay alive and awake and keep our eyes open for enchantment.

I've spent most of my adult life searching for this kind of enchantment and going to the furthest reaches of the planet to find it. But, as the past three years have proven, the wonder I've been seeking has been right here all along. Inside my brain and my body, in the way I see and experience all of life, wherever I am on Earth.

Delight, wonder, enchantment, awe – it's all around us, all of the time, and is the very thing that will ultimately push us to act. We just have to learn to pay attention, stay alert to the tears and the goosebumps that let us know the transcendent and the sacred are near, and slow down enough to do that.

It's in the light as it catches in the gum leaves, in the rain hanging off a spider's web, in the silence that wraps around us when we're walking through the bush. It's in the kookaburras cackling at dawn, in the breeze sliding past the backs of our knees on a summer's day, in the thrum of cicadas at dusk. It's in the smiles of the people we love, in sea foam and soil, in wild weeds and tree trunks. And, yes, in psychedelic rainbow jelly combs blobbing about in the ocean, just waiting for us to notice them.

A Short Note on the Way Forward

So much has changed in the past four years since that fateful trip to the Arctic. My life, like so many of our lives, has been entirely remoulded by Covid-19, by fire and by flood, and by the internal and external journeys I've been on over that time. I am a different me to the me who visited the polar bears in Churchill. And I'm certainly a different me to the me who happily hopscotched around the world, chasing one ecstatic high after another, the hungry ghost always in search of escape.

Since turning down that private jet trip in Africa, I have said a lot of nos. I've said no to quick overseas jaunts to review day spas, to two-day trips across the other side of the country, to cruises on mega ships that give little back to the communities they visit while taking a lot from the environment, and many more.

There are, however, still full body yeses. To assignments and trips that not only help me pay the bills, but also align with my aim of spreading the message of travelling in a way that helps rather than hinders the communities and places we visit. It's an ongoing journey to figure out how to do this, and I know I'll continue tripping up along the way, but the point is that I'm trying. The point is that we all keep trying, until there is no breath left in our lungs.

My guidelines now are quite simple. Get very clear on where I want to go and why. If there isn't a good enough reason to go, stay and continue becoming more deeply embedded in the land I'm from, and therefore a better custodian of it. Go to places closer to home, remembering all the magic that can be discovered in our own corners of the world, and once or twice a year somewhere further afield if I can stay for a decent amount of time and do some meaningful work there, especially places that need tourist dollars. Support businesses there that are locally owned, prioritise Indigenous guides who are the rightful stewards of the lands I'm visiting, and leave the place at least as well as I found it, if not better. And when I get home, tell stories that will help readers rethink the way they travel, and spread the word about important issues these places are facing.

If you picked this book up and made it to the end, chances are you too are a mindful traveller, or at least aspire to be one. So maybe it's time for you to define your own set of mindful travel parameters, remembering that every choice we make matters and that we all have an ecological role to play on this earth. This might mean deciding never to get on a plane again, or being part of a social impact project in your destination whenever you do, or getting crystal clear on your purpose for each trip. It might mean putting the natural world at the centre of your travels by weaving, hiking or camping into them, or travelling less regularly and more slowly when you do, opening yourself up wide to gratitude and awe and wonder.

Whatever you decide to do, travelling this way can be a form of activism. One that can fill you up and help you like who you are when you look in the mirror, while also respecting our earth and making it a better planet to live on. It's really the very least we can do.

Acknowledgements

I offer deep gratitude to every place mentioned in this book for inspiring my career, work and personal philosophies, and more importantly to the traditional custodians of those places, who continue to caretake their forests, waters and soils for generations to come.

This book is the product of a lifetime of travels and wouldn't exist without the support of the publications I write for and their editors, chief among them Lauren Quaintance, Anthony Dennis and Fiona Carruthers. Some of the chapters in this book began their life as travel stories in the *Sydney Morning Herald*'s *Traveller*, the *Australian Financial Review*'s *Life & Leisure* and *Condé Nast Traveller*. I am thankful for those and all other commissions.

Thank you to the dynamic team at Affirm Press, especially my publisher Kelly Doust. You believed in this book from the beginning, have shown deep sensitivity, commitment and passion, and have helped me bring forth something that is so expressive of my love for the world. Thank you to the wonderfully kind Elizabeth Robinson-Griffith for her editing skills, to Anna Thwaites for her sharp eye and to Emma Schwarcz for taking care of the finer details. You have all strengthened this book in important ways.

Endless gratitude to Jenny Fran Davis at Verto Literary for seeing the larger narrative arc of this book when I could not, and for identifying the places where I wasn't reaching a deeper level of truth. I would have been lost without you. And to my brilliant agent Jane Novak for her advocacy and determination, thank you.

To the team at Groundswell Giving, especially Arielle Gamble: thank you for inviting me to the Heron Island Fellowship where I could clearly see the purpose of this book and my work moving forward, and for providing a constant reminder that together, we really can make a difference.

To the owners of Happy Sun House and Wildwood Church, who hosted me for writing retreats, and to my gorgeous friends Sahar Zadah, Ellie Waterhouse and Laura May Gibbs, thank you for opening your homes for me to write in when we were out of ours.

Thank you to my other-life sisters, Nathalie Kelley and Amy Tuxworth, for being my creative mirrors, and for your unique perspectives, encouragement and laughter. Also to Jess and Jasmine for those Monday-morning brainstorming sessions.

To my mum and dad, Mary and Stan Karnikowski, thank you for being living examples of good earth custodianship since 1984, and to Mum especially for always being such a fierce champion of my work. No one but you would save every article I have ever written. Most of all, thank you to my joyful, twinkly, tender, loving husband, Peter Windrim: you are my *anam cara* and my forever first reader, and your laughter and tears tell me when my writing is finally getting there. You're right: we are lit by the same light.

To the ecologists, travel writers and poets who are the lamps by which I write, thank you – especially Joanna Macy, Helena Norberg-Hodge, Pico Iyer, Robin Wall Kimmerer, Thích Nhất Hạnh, Rachel Carson, Mary Oliver, Bob Brown, Jane Goodall, Leigh Ann Henion, Pema Chödrön and Wendell Berry. Your thoughts have illuminated mine in powerful ways.

Finally, to this spinning planet we all call home: we haven't done a good job of looking after you in recent decades, but there are more and more of us standing up and fighting to keep you as abundant and astonishingly beautiful as you are. What an honour it is to serve you.